GOD AND CAPITALISM
A Prophetic Critique
of Market Economy

Essays by
Norman K. Gottwald
William K. Tabb
Beverly W. Harrison
Gregory Baum
Dorothee Soelle

Edited by
J. Mark Thomas and Vernon Visick

D0217390

A-R Editions, Inc.
Madison, Wisconsin

Library of Congress Cataloging-in-Publication Data

God and capitalism : a prophetic critique of market economy : essays /
   by Norman K. Gottwald . . . [et al.] ; edited by J. Mark Thomas and
   Vernon Visick.
       p.   cm.
   Includes bibliographical references.
   ISBN 0-89579-251-6
   1. Capitalism—Religious aspects—Christianity—Controversial
literature.   2. Capitalism—Religious aspects—Judaism—
Controversial literature.   3. Judaism—Doctrines.   4. Free
enterprise.   I. Gottwald, Norman K. (Norman Karol), 1926-
II. Thomas, J. Mark, 1947-   . III. Visick, Vernon.
BR115.C3G63   1990
261.8′5—dc20   90-41601
                                                                          CIP

The quotation on page 31 is reprinted with permission of *Christianity &
Crisis*, 537 W. 121st Street, New York, NY 10027, copyright 1987.

Unless otherwise indicated, scripture quotations are from the Revised
Standard Version of the Bible, copyright 1946, 1952, 1971 by the Division
of Christian Education of the National Council of Churches of Christ in
the USA and are used by permission.

A-R Editions, Inc.
801 Deming Way
Madison, Wisconsin 53717
(608) 836-9000   FAX (608) 831-8200

10 9 8 7 6 5 4 3 2 1

Contents

This volume of essays
is affectionately dedicated
to the memory of
Liesl Blockstein
who in her life and work
lived in the spirit of the prophets.

*"She opens her arms to the poor
and extends her hands to the needy."*

Proverbs 31:20

Introduction

The Quest for
Economic Justice

J. Mark Thomas
Senior Research Fellow
Au Sable Institute of Environmental Studies

"How can security and a decent standard of life for all be
attained according to the infinite productive power of mankind,
without the complete mechanization and dehumanization of [hu-
man beings]?" Paul Tillich's question concerning economic justice
at the end of the Second World War remains distressingly contemporary as the century draws to a close. While the war left
buildings and institutions in ruins and millions homeless and
hungry, the contemporary world lets 43,000 children die each day
of hunger, while millions live on the margins of human existence.
This occurs not in the context of international war or depression,
but in that of a world wherein economic indicators are up, international investors trade in the billions of dollars, energy and food
are abundant, and the concentration of wealth at the top is
increasing.[1] What is the moral meaning of this situation?

First, it must be admitted that the ethical question itself has not always been welcome in the contemporary economic debate. It has been objected that ethicists have no business in economic disputes; they lack the expertise to add anything but naive opinions to complex problems. Tillich was aware of such complaints, and he confessed that "Christianity cannot offer technical advice for economic planning." But then, he noted, the technical problems of economic theory had been thoroughly studied already. "The problem of an economic system able to give security of permanent full employment and certainty of decent livelihood for all is much more largely in the realms of political and moral decisions," realms wherein religious principles are "decisive."[2] The problems of full employment, common economic security, access to necessary goods, the responsible use of resources, and the humane organization of productive forces are finally problems of social ethics. They are economic matters only in their technical elements. In essence they are questions of distributive justice that cannot be answered by economic reasoning as such. Yet, the way they are solved reveals what societies intend to do with persons and groups. Every economic system is simultaneously a system of distributive justice and a moral statement about the right relationship between liberty and equality, the distribution of rewards and punishments, and the relation between persons and community and between stability and change.

If economic theory attempts to prescribe the ultimate ends of human existence—of what persons and communities essentially are and ought to be—it becomes a religious ethic, making implicit claims about ultimate meaning (religion) and value (ethics). If religion attempts to prescribe technical means for accomplishing economic ends, it becomes a poor competitor to that "dismal science," lacking the systematic tools to accomplish its purposes. In brief, economics can say nothing meaningful about its final ends, and religion can say nothing sensible about instrumental means. From this perspective, a "Christian economics" or a "capitalist faith" are equally nonsensical. Both represent an unwarranted hegemony beyond the reach of their proper objects and methods.

Still, two contemporary movements have claimed a special relationship between Christianity and capitalism. Representatives of the neoconservative movement such as Michael Novak, Robert Benne, and Richard Neuhaus argue that there is a particular coherence between the Christian and capitalist understandings of human nature. Both are ultimately realistic about the human condition of self-interestedness. Novak celebrates this moral realism in the current economic arrangements: "Democratic capitalism was in the mind of its first theoreticians a marvelously designed method for harnessing the energies of human self-interest and selfishness for social purposes. There seems to be no question that this design has been successful."[3] Democratic capitalism accords not to the best ideals of the most utopian thinkers, the neoconservatives argue, but to the realism of a Christian understanding of human nature. Capitalism may not fit in a perfect world, but it represents the best hope for the real world of individual desire and action. Because Christianity does not romanticize human goodness, it offers no blueprint for utopia. Unlike those progressive souls who want to engineer a perfect system, Christianity understands the pervasiveness and the endurance of human sin. Thus, if democratic capitalism is not a perfect system, and if it does not articulate the most high-minded of ethical positions, it remains the best of all possible *imperfect* systems, approximating most closely the goods dreamed of by its competitors.[4]

The coherence between Christianity and capitalism discovered by the new religious right is less nuanced than that of the neoconservatives. Like the German Christians before them who argued that the "orders" of life were ordained of God,[5] the new religious right argues that American institutions are direct expressions of the will of God—at least in origin. The most visible representative of this movement, Jerry Falwell, demonstrates this political theology in a set of staccato assertions:

> The free-enterprise system is clearly outlined in the Book of Proverbs in the Bible. Jesus Christ made it clear that the work ethic was a part of His plan for man. Ownership of property is biblical. Competition in business is biblical. Ambitious and successful business management is clearly outlined as a part of God's plan for His people.[6]

While neoconservatives consider moral criticism of the international market system to be utopian, the new religious right regards it is an act of rebellion against God. While the neoconservatives press the argument on the ground of a "realistic" philosophical theology, the new religious right depends upon a selective and literalistic biblicism. Both movements affirm the intimate connection between religion and the American political economy beyond the familiar motivational, individual success motif. At the turn of the century, Russell Conwell claimed that "to make money honestly is to preach the gospel."[7] While the gospel of success continues to be a popular motif in American religious life, it is not identical to the broader social and political claims of neoconservatism and the new religious right.

Both of these political theologies covet the historical high ground, that of "conserving" American origins. However, they generally disregard that American vision of the social and personal good represented by the oldest of American Christian traditions. The Puritans of New England would and did punish behavior that the American right assumes to be traditional economic virtue. The Boston merchant Robert Keayne was tried and admonished "in the name of the Church for selling his wares at excessive rates, to the dishonor of God's name, the offence of the General Court, and the public scandal of the country." A pair of stocks on the Boston commons first restrained their maker, who charged the community more than a "just price" for them. A laissez-faire capitalist (had such a person existed) would have been consigned to the criminal classes in Puritan New England. There was no tolerance yet in the "New Jerusalem" for the morality of Wall Street. The novel ethic of commerce would have to wait for what sociologist Robert Bellah has called "the broken covenant." The earliest American vision of public morality was that of Puritan New England, and the New Deal came closer to approximating it than the New Federalism of the Reagan administration.

If this founding national tradition is not being "conserved" by American neoconservatism, neither is the classical tradition most commonly associated with the name. Aristotle knew nothing of capitalism, of course; it is strictly a product of modernity. But he did know something of the drive to accumulate money without any apparent end, and it puzzled him. Why would anybody want to do that? It "may be that they are eager for life but not for the good life," he speculated. "These people turn all skills into skills of acquiring goods, as though that were the end and everything had to serve that end." But it is contrary to nature and reason to make the *means* of life into its *ends*. And most unnatural of all for Aristotle is the acquiring of goods by the charging of interest and the exchange of goods for profit. Thus, he summarizes, the "acquisition of goods is . . . of two kinds; one, which is necessary and approved of, is to do with household-management; the other, which is to do with trade and depends on exchange, is justly regarded with disapproval, since it arises not from nature but from men's gaining from each other."[8] There is nothing apparently "neoclassical" about the political economics of the neoconservatives and hence nothing "conservative," as this has been traditionally understood in the West.

If the classical tradition is not manifest in the criticisms and programs of the new religious right and the neoconservatives, the biblical tradition is yet claimed as a grounding reality. "We must . . . have a return to biblical basics," laments Jerry Falwell.[9] And former President Reagan has attested to the "incontrovertible fact that all the complex and horrendous questions confronting us at home and worldwide have their answers in that single book."[10] But do the political economics of these movements reflect the biblical tradition of economic justice? The prophet Amos speaks:

> Listen to this, you who trample on the needy
> and try to suppress the poor people of the country,
> you who say "When will New Moon be over
> so that we can sell our corn,
> and sabbath, so that we can market our wheat?
> Then by lowering the bushel, raising the shekel,
> by swindling and tampering with the scales,
> we can buy up the poor for money,
> and the needy for a pair of sandals,
> and get a price even for the sweepings of the wheat."
> Yahweh swears it by the pride of Jacob,
> "Never will I forget a single thing that you have done."
> Is this not the reason for the earthquakes,
> for its inhabitants all mourning,
> and all of it heaving, like the Nile,
> then subsiding, like the river of Egypt?
> (Amos 8:4–8, *The Jerusalem Bible*)

Amos portrayed the God of history and nature as being enraged by economic injustice. But why should the transcendent God of creation be concerned with the mundane business of getting and spending wealth? The answer is that economic life—and every other form of social organization—is a matter of justice, and justice is close to God's heart. "It is because God is the source of justice that His pathos is ethical," explains Abraham Heschel, "and it is because God is absolutely personal . . . that this ethos is full of pathos."[11] God's response to injustice is anger, say the prophets, even when this injustice is perpetrated by God's own chosen people. And here is perhaps the crux of the difference between a "conservative" political theology and a "prophetic" one. While "culture religion"—as Reinhold Niebuhr called it—confirms the ideals of national existence, prophetic religion measures self, friend, and foe against the same plumb line of justice. This moral universalism, as Paul Tillich and Mircea Eliade have argued, is what makes prophetic Judaism unique in history. There is no holy space safe from the demand of justice. It matters ultimately that righteousness characterize economic relations, and no economic system is beyond criticism.

The five essays in this volume apply "prophetic criticism" to contemporary problems of economic justice. In this, they follow a line of theological thought developed in the first half of the century by the religious socialisms of Paul Tillich and Reinhold Niebuhr. More proximately, the context for these conversations has been set by the quest for a "just, participatory, and sustainable society" carried on in the dialogues of the World Council of Churches, by the American bishops' pastoral letter on the economy, and by the movement of "liberation theology" generally. In all three of these important developments there is criticism of current international economic arrangements and a call for greater economic justice. Each of the contributions in this volume manifests an especially close identification with liberation theology. Thus, they begin their reflections upon ultimate meaning and value from the perspective of the poor.

Considering the context for the rise of the prophets in ancient Israel, biblical scholar Norman Gottwald argues that there is an intimate relationship between the ethics of the prophets and a "communitarian" form of economic life. The prophetic ethic, he claims, emerged from the Semitic underclass who lived at the mercy of the region's great city-states, which thrived on an economics of "conscription." The prophets apply the "communitarian" ethic of this underclass to a prosperous kingship which has returned to conscription and exploitation. "Arising in opposition to a foreign tributary mode of production—or one that became 'foreign' to them as they withdrew from it—they now returned to a native tributary mode of production." If prophetic Judaism and Christianity now contend with forms of economic conscription, it is because this criticism reaches back to the very root of the historical faith.

A different story is told among the neoconservatives, economist William Tabb indicates. Irving Kristol, for instance, "seems to be saying that the rabbinical tradition . . . has . . . locked up the prophetic writings—and has allowed them to be read only by those who have been inoculated by status quo realism." But Tabb's own experience in synagogue and among liberation theologians articulates quite a different vision. Prophetic Judaism is faithful Judaism and is antithetical to the calculating methods of the neoconservatives. It is an ethical passion at war with an unjust status quo. And this worldwide status quo, Tabb indicates, is one wherein wealth accumulates toward the top while the poor— including the new working poor—fall farther and farther behind. That massive poverty and unemployment are not inevitable is demonstrated by Tabb's review of the evidence comparing national policies on employment. The Scandinavian countries do particularly well in this regard. But there are indications of a new class conflict breaking down that ideological line separating the neoconservative and the prophetic understandings of justice and equality.

Fundamentally agreeing with Tabb's class analysis, Christian ethicist Beverly Harrison attempts to break normative social theory out of its "mainstream" and "malestream" captivity. She advocates a "radical" position wherein neoclassical economics is seen as an ideology, embodying an implicit ethical and theological system. From her "socialist-feminist liberation hermeneutic," Harrison catalogues the effects of the political economy on the middle classes, including the creation of powerlessness, the breaking up of families, downward mobility, and the exhaustion of the common good. The political economy tends to centralize wealth and power within and between nations, excluding from its privileged strata those who lie outside the norm of white, heterosexual, First World males. With the prosperity of post-war America on the wane, Harrison believes that the time has come for the "democratization" of economic life.

Moral theologian and social theorist Gregory Baum reflects upon the political economy from a Canadian perspective. Reviewing the teachings on economic life by the Catholic church and especially the Canadian bishops, Baum discovers a critical tradition running counter to the neoconservative trend. In various contemporary documents, the church has come to understand the dynamics of capitalism in terms of "imperialism," the centralization of power in the transnational corporations, the internationalization of capital, deindustrialization, unemployment, and economic dependency. The Canadian bishops, for instance, "do not regard monetarism as the dominant philosophy guiding the political economy," but as a "disguise." Rather than being disinterested observers, governments are deeply involved in creating the conditions for the continued power of the transnationals. This situation is buttressed by national ideologies that make capitalism patriotic and continue the Cold War in the name of "national security." Finally, Baum contrasts the methodologies of the American and Canadian bishops' letters on the economy: the Americans begin with moral theological principles and move to concrete problems; the Canadians begin with the problems of the political economy and move toward principles. The results of such a critical inquiry have been widely appreciated by persons with an "emancipatory commitment," who are eager to move society toward greater justice.

In the concluding essay by Christian social ethicist Dorothee Soelle, the conversation comes back full circle to scripture. What is "God's economy," God's will for our economic life? Soelle finds a paradigm for an answer in the Jewish tradition of the Jubilee Year. All of the Sabbath regulations—including the Jubilee tradition—depend upon the understanding that the earth is not our own but the Lord's. Thus, the biblical perspective stands in stark contrast to the capitalist notion of property. The earth is God's. "The poor understand this immediately: the earth is not the property of the United Fruit Company, nor of Standard Oil, nor of the Somoza clan." Parallel to this contrast is that between two competing confessions: a "theology of the bourgeoisie" and a "theology of liberation." Characteristic of bourgeois theology are its individualism and its social location among the "white, relatively wealthy, male-run, and . . . androcentricly thinking middle class." Liberation theology, in contrast, originates with communities of the poor and seeks the transformation of life. And Soelle identifies the direction of this change as toward the "equality of the use and distribution of goods." Humans are equal in needs, these Sabbath traditions indicate, but today the biblical attitude is denounced as "communist." If the biblical tradition is considered to be utopian, this may show how estranged we have become, for we can no longer even dream our dreams. A faithful reading of the Bible must come through the eyes of the poor, concludes Soelle, and in the equalizing economy God will liberate all from the rule of the powers and the principalities.

Of course, any good conversation generates as many questions as it answers. These five essays do no less. The problem of the relationship between culture and religion is probably a perennial one. But these five thinkers crack the neoconservative hegemony in theology. They provide strong arguments for what H. Richard Niebuhr called a tranformational ethic. In this way, they provide a direct challenge to those theologies of culture articulated by the neoconservatives and the new religious right. The identity between the American way of life and the kingdom of God is certainly broken. Justice is at the heart of theological ethics and it can be measured only by the yardstick of the poor, these essays insist. Long after the historical situation described in these essays has changed, this prophetic perspective will endure.

---

[1]A study for the Federal Reserve indicated that in 1982 .5 percent of the American people held 35 percent of the wealth, and that in the twenty previous years, all other groups had lost wealth.

[2]Paul Tillich, *The Spiritual Situation in Our Technical Society*, ed. J. Mark Thomas (Macon, Georgia: Mercer University Press, 1988), 20.

[3]Michael Novak, *The American Vision: An Essay on the Future of Democratic Capitalism* (Washington, D.C.: American Enterprise Institute for Public Policy Research, 1978), 13.

[4]Novak answers the notion of Gregory Baum that "sinful structures" have evil effects independent of the intentions of those who work within them by pointing out that "systems may also produce good independently of the personal intentions of those who work in them. This was Adam Smith's point about 'the natural system of liberty.' The intentions of individual workers may, or may not, be noble; yet the cumulative effect of their actions, if the

system is well designed, may be to produce the wealth of nations" (Michael Novak, *The Spirit of Democratic Capitalism* [New York: Simon and Schuster and American Enterprise Institute, 1982], 285). With the collapse of Eastern European Communism and the longing for democracy there, neoconservatism has turned triumphalist. Francis Fukuyama, for instance, asks Hegel's question concerning whether the West has now reached a set of social relationships beyond the contradictions of history and answers with an undialectical yes. What is humanly possible has been achieved in Western liberal societies and cannot be transcended in the direction of justice (Francis Fukuyama, "The End of History?" *The National Interest* [Summer 1989]: 3–35).

[5]Cf. J. Mark Thomas, "The Resurgence of Religious Nationalism," *Encounter* 47 (Spring 1986): 127–142.

[6]Jerry Falwell, *Listen America!* (Garden City, New York: Doubleday, 1980), 13.

[7]Russell H. Conwell, *Acres of Diamonds* (Westwood, New Jersey: Revell, 1960), 24.

[8]Aristotle, *The Politics*, trans. T. A. Sinclair, rev. Trevor J. Saunders (Harmondsworth, Middlesex, England: Penguin Books), 81–87.

[9]Falwell, *Listen America!*, 18.

[10]"Reagan Backs Evangelicals in Their Political Activities," *New York Times*, 23 August 1980, sec. 1, 8.

[11]Abraham J. Heschel, *The Prophets* (New York: Harper & Row, 1962), 2, 5.

CHAPTER 1

From Tribal Existence to Empire: The Socio-Historical Context for the Rise of the Hebrew Prophets

Norman Gottwald
Professor of Biblical Studies
New York Theological Seminary

Is there a biblical perspective on economics? This is both an ethical and a historical question, and neither question can be answered properly without also addressing the other. Ethically, it is recognized that the Bible calls for economic "justice." But biblical economic justice remains a vague generalization unless biblical economic systems can be recognized—and that is where the historical analysis becomes relevant.

Normally, not much thought is given to the historical nature of economic systems. Still, it is worth noting that the economic system of the United States is at most two hundred years old, and it undergoes considerable changes every fifty years or so. It is certainly not an eternal system, although it has been portrayed that way by its most ardent defenders. Thus, a historical view of how economies have come to be the way they are provides a much needed perspective in contemplating economic change.

In addition, Jews and Christians should have an interest in the views of economics expressed in the Bible. Some Jews and Christians argue that religion has little or nothing to do with economics and that if there were a dominant economic system favored in the Bible it would be irrelevant today because so much has changed since then. A review of biblical history sharply qualifies both of these arguments, particularly if the focus is placed on the prophetic movement and the socioeconomic structural context in which prophecy arose. The central question to be explored can be put in this way: Is there a biblical economics that is prescriptive, obligatory, or in any way exemplary for Jews and Christians today? The answer developed here is basically that the Bible will not solve our economic problems, but that knowledge of its economics is necessary if religious resources are to be called upon to deal with economics intelligently. The prophets will be used to suggest a concrete, working solution to this thorny question.

Some of the categories to be applied in this analysis are not often used in biblical interpretation. One such concept is "political economy," which can be described as the means by which people produce and reproduce their lives. Political economy has to do with how we keep ourselves going from day to day, develop our social relations, assert and accept authority, and generate ways of thinking about what we are doing. These thought patterns concern the way the system works, from provision for the most elementary needs, such as getting food and shelter, to the notions entertained about the ultimate meaning of life. This essay will inquire into the forms of political economy in ancient Israel as reflected in the Bible.

Another key concept is that of "labor," the outlay of human energy that is required for the maintenance of life. The simplest requirements for life must be satisfied before higher cultural products can be created. Labor and the labor product encompass all human productions from foodstuffs and clothing to works of art and religious faith. Among the products of such labor are written texts, including the biblical books. The political economy of biblical times is therefore expressed in various kinds of labor products generated by people living in those times, including their religious ideas, practices, and texts.

Within this process of production, another concept of importance is that of "power relations." These relations among people determine the volume and flow of labor products: who decides what gets produced and who benefits from the use of what is produced. Only by learning something about the power struggles that went on in biblical communities is it possible to discern their economic system and to estimate its connection with the so-called market economics of modernity. A key aspect of power in all situations is who has the means to "explain" or "interpret" what is happening in the society, so that their view of political economy (including how labor is applied according to prevailing power relations) is accepted as correct. Power conflict is often a struggle over correct ideas, as is amply demonstrated in the Bible.

The major form of production in the ancient world in which Israel arose has been called "tributary."[1] The tributary form of production was pre-capitalist: it did not involve capital formation in anything like the modern sense. But it did include relationships of domination, and the structure of that power system was bipolar: a powerful central state (such as Egypt, Assyria, or Babylon) or a smaller city-state (such as Canaan or Syria) dominated a considerable stretch of land made up largely of villages engaged in agriculture and animal breeding. These villages contained up to 98 percent of the state's population. Peasants had "use ownership" of the land, but the state claimed entitlement to tax the villages first in the form of payment in kind and second in the form of conscription of labor for public works or army service. So the state regularly intruded into the village communities and took a good part of their labor products. Many peasants, already living on the margin, were further impoverished and driven into debt by these measures. Many were compelled to take loans at staggering interest rates offered by a money-lending merchant and absentee-landlord class that grew up with state blessing and support. While not precisely comparable in all respects, the political economies of many Third World countries today exhibit features very much like this tributary pattern in the ancient Near East. This helps to explain why Bible readers in Third World countries are often quicker to grasp the stark realities of biblical economics than those of us in more protected economic environments where inequities and hardships are less blatant. This also helps to explain why Third World peasants and workers can grasp the fundamentals of a liberation theology that baffles First World intellectuals.

Israel arose within the tributary political economy just described, and it did so in a very unusual way.[2] There is something notably different about the religion of the Bible, and it is definitely connected with the peculiarity of its earliest political economy. What is unusual about the first communities of Israelites is that they did not give or take tribute. They refused allegiance to the states that taxed and conscripted their subjects, and they themselves strove not to extract tribute from one another. These first Israelites were residents of the small villages in the highlands of Canaan, and they banded together in large families and tribes to protect themselves from the Canaanite city-states and ultimately from the Egyptian empire.

Simply expressed, earliest Israel was in rebellion against the tributary system and the political and religious arrangements that legitimated and enforced it. These people of the new deity Yahweh were not willing to pay taxes, to be conscripted into the city-state armies, or to be debt-obligated. They asserted the full and free use of their own labor products, and they did so within the context of a society and culture where cooperation took precedence over competition.

How was their emphatic break with the all-powerful tributary system achieved? Israel attributed this "new beginning" to her delivering God. Historically, however, the factors that contributed to this deliverance must be sought. One way of understanding what happened is that the Canaanite city-states were weakening and in virtual collapse. No doubt this was true. Yet the books of Joshua and Judges (which, though written much later, contain earlier traditions) contain significant indications that these assertive peasants were taking advantage of weaknesses in the political system and joining together in the common cause of becoming free agrarians. In particular, they developed their own distinctive measures of self-help, cooperative labor, and mutual aid, extending assistance from one family or clan to another, making grants-in-aid that passed among the people without interest charges. They also created their own culture, and it is especially through their religious culture—which they passed on to Western society—that we know these Israelites best. It is the specific contention of this analysis that Israel's religion can be understood adequately only when it is seen as an important dimension of Israel's political economy.

The Hebrew language appears to have been a dialect of the Canaanite language. It was apparently the dialect of the under-class Canaanites who became Israelites, mostly cultivators of the soil, but including pastoral nomads, artisans, and priests. They emerged bit by bit as a new people whose ethnic identity was formed in the midst of their struggle to establish themselves firmly in the hill country of western Palestine. The difficulty in saying exactly what it meant to be "Israelite" at the time stems from the fact that Israel was just then coming into being. Later on, what it meant to be "Jewish," especially in the midst of geograph-ical dispersion and political domination, was shaped in good mea-sure by Israel's original background of political and economic resistance to the overwhelming power of the state and its wealthy and privileged clients.[3]

The exodus from Egypt served as a metaphor to describe all kinds of experiences of oppression and resistance shared by the Canaan Israelites, who had to contend not only with the Canaan-ite city-states, but also with the Philistines, Medianites, Ammo-nites, and Moabites, as well as the Egyptians, who exerted an imperial claim over Canaan. One could fairly say, therefore, that every Israelite group had its own experience of a pharaoh and an exodus. When early Israel speaks in legend or saga about those delivering experiences under Moses or Joshua, the historicity of the events lies not so much in details of time and place as in testimony to the process of social and political struggle by which Israel emerged from disparate groups of politically and econom-ically subject peoples. There is a pattern of community formation that runs through these diverse, sometimes fanciful, traditions: Israel, under tributary oppression, resists and is delivered into a new communitarian society that it strives to sustain through cov-enant and law.[4]

How did the religion of Israel fit within the situation just described? A striking feature of the traditions from the very start is that the God of this people, known as Yahweh, is distinctively a delivering God who takes a strong stand on behalf of the op-pressed underclasses that compose Israel. God creates a people out of those who were counted as no people according to the estimate of the political and economic leaders of the time. Yahweh not only sets these former "nobodies" on a new foundation that gives them identity and self-worth, but grants them alternative social and economic forms of life so that they need not lapse back into tributary domination or be torn apart by unbridled self-seeking. Very roughly, this may be called a "communitarian" mode of production in contrast to the tributary mode of production from which Israel dissented and withdrew and against which it had to defend itself.

To be sure, this communitarian mode of production did not prevail once Israel itself became a monarchic state with its own kings. And it was this turn to monarchy that set the stage for Israel's prophets to appear. The rise of Israelite monarchy is usually explained by Israel's military need to unify its forces in order to defeat the Philistines, who were a more formidable enemy than the divided Canaanite city-states had been. But the return of Israel to a tributary system was probably more complicated than that. Power struggles within the tribes probably weakened the communitarian manner of life, especially the judicial system designed to secure even-handed preservation of rights. Families that had prospered on particularly good land seem to have used their influence to press for strengthened state power under David and Solomon. The communitarian spirit and practice of the people did not disappear overnight, but now it was dominated and threatened by Israelite state power.

What this means is that within about two centuries the Israelite tribes had gone full circle. Arising in opposition to a foreign tributary mode of production—or one that became "foreign" to them as they withdrew from it—they now returned to a native tributary mode of production. One could say that they were now able to be ruled and oppressed by Israelite kings, merchants, and landlords instead of by non-Israelites. But many Israelites found no consolation in the fact that they were now oppressed by fellow Israelites instead of outsiders. Indeed, it struck many as an affront to and violation of their history and constitution as a communitarian people. Precisely this ironic situation is played upon by many of the prophets, some of whom came to prefer the prospect of foreign oppression to continued exploitation by Israelite kings and upper classes.

At any rate, the practical result for political economy was that a three-cornered conflict developed.[5] The villages did not simply disappear. The Israelite state did not suddenly urbanize in the way that modern industrializing states have been able to do. The economy continued to consist of fundamentally small-scale agriculture organized by village networks. But the key political decision making was vested in the Israelite monarchy, and this meant taxing and conscripting policies, without which the state could not have thrived and taken its place among the other ancient Near East states. It also meant coercing peasants into growing lucrative export crops, a policy that often exacted a heavy sacrifice in the peasants' own standard of living and capacity to survive.

Alongside the state and the agrarian populace, coexisting in uneasy tension that sometimes broke into open conflict, was a third power: the foreign tributary mode of production that became an increasing threat both to the Israelite state and to its peasant subjects. Foreign conquerors began to exact tribute and indemnities from Israel, and these payments had to come out of the same Israelite villages that paid taxes to Jerusalem or Samaria (double taxation without representation!). Eventually Assyria wiped out the northern kingdom of Israel, and Babylonia overthrew the southern kingdom of Judah. Israel's experiment in monarchic statehood had died. Henceforth, except for less than a century under the Hasmonean dynasty, the descendants of the Israelite tribes and states were a people subject to other powers. After Babylonia came Persia, the Hellenistic empires, and Rome. But by this time the Israelite people (now identified as Jewish) had developed such a distinctive culture and religion that they survived with remarkable tenacity, integrity, and flexibility, even when restricted by colonial servitude. This culture, known now as Judaism, has continued in its main contours to the present day.

Although not strictly called for in the scope of this essay, a word should be said about Jesus and political economy. This is necessary because Christians are inclined to think that Jesus led a solely ethical and spiritual movement that had little or nothing to do with social and economic conditions. This is an entirely mistaken notion. The location of the work of Jesus and of the Jesus movement in Palestine—before Christianity became a primarily Gentile faith—was in alignment with the communitarian values and practices of the countryside of Galilee. This placed Jesus in opposition to the native tributary power represented by the Sadducees and the Jewish elite in Jerusalem and ultimately to the foreign tributary power of Rome. The strategy of Jesus and his movement seems to have been to aim at the Jewish elite and the temple economy rather than to target Rome directly. It was this Jewish elite and temple economy that imposed native tributary servitude on the people, while it simultaneously served Roman interests. The clearest single piece of historical information about Jesus is that he died as a political provocateur or disturber of that "alliance of convenience" between the Roman and the Jewish tributary modes of production.

This sketch of the place of Jesus in the political economy of his time is crucial for Christian reasoning about biblical economics and contemporary economics alike. It means, for instance, that discussion about whether or not Jesus was violent, politically speaking, is a red herring, since to answer positively or negatively ignores substantive questions about the politics of Jesus. He was implicated in politics of a communitarian stripe, whatever his precise methods were or whatever he thought he was accomplishing. He was killed for primarily political reasons. His followers went on to live in various relations and accommodations to political economies in Palestine and throughout the Roman Empire. The interconnection of religion and political economy was from the beginning as intimate and inescapable for Christians as for Jews, and the same is true today. Religion and political economy cannot simply be pulled apart and regarded in isolation. That is not only a general principle that can be illustrated from many known religions; it is concretely demonstrated in the provocative, controversial stance of Jesus toward his own society.[6]

Attention should be turned now to the ancient Israelite prophets who were active during the time of the independent Israelite kingdoms and into the period of Babylonian and Persian domination of the Jews. It clearly does not do the prophets justice to see them as foretellers of predetermined events or as teachers of ethics or theology in a formal or scholastic sense. They are more nearly commentators, analysts, and critics of the social and religious orders. The prophetic movement is a long-sustained exploration and criticism of how the tributary mode of production permeates and distorts Israelite (and later Jewish) culture and religion. For the most part the prophets do not evaluate society from an abstract position of religious doctrine, mysticism, or spirituality, but from the perspective of the communitarian mode of production and its values. These had become well defined in the time of the judges and still existed in the village communities throughout Palestine. All the developments in later Israelite history that jeopardize this communitarian mode of life are severely judged by the prophets. To state it religiously, prophetic theology and ethics are unrelentingly communitarian in their conception of what God wants of human beings.[7]

Not all the prophets came from villages or from the ranks of the poor, to be sure. Some may have been from higher echelons of society, just as throughout history advocates of the unprivileged have come from higher classes. These prophets were troubled by the chauvinist and elitist assumptions about Israelite superiority to other peoples and about the virtues and wisdom of established rulers. They exposed smug self-righteousness and narrow self-interest in the politically and socially powerful who claimed to be serving Israel as a whole. They turned a pitiless eye on the inhuman effects of national leadership on the majority of ordinary Israelites. They foresaw the ruin of the nation through internal spoliation and external conquest.

How truly "practical" or "realistic" the prophetic criticisms actually were is a serious question, and this same uncertainty haunts attempts to apply their analyses (even by loose analogy) to modern societies. The political leaders of Israel and Judah had a number of understandable objections to these prophets; sometimes these objections are voiced in the Bible. Yet it is clear that Israelite leaders were not more evil than other leaders in tributary systems of political economy. To make their systems thrive and to keep control as leaders they felt compelled to maintain tax policies and launch building and military programs that were humanly very costly to their subjects. These same leaders also felt themselves entitled to privilege and luxury. The difference in the prophetic outlook was that the prophets were measuring present performance by communitarian rather than tributary standards, which meant that they felt compelled to represent the welfare of the majority of Israelites, who did not have entree or voice in the royal court or in the circles of the powerful merchants and land-grabbers. In particular, the prophets were caustic about the way judicial verdicts and religious blessings were obtainable virtually on demand, if one had enough money or favors to dispense to judges, priests, or prophets "for hire."

So, in substance, most of the prophets were quarreling with aspects of a tributary political economy, as practiced by Israelite leaders and foreign powers, that threatened the communitarian integrity of the people. And because they saw the religion of Yahweh rooted in the old covenantal, communitarian style of life, with its mutual commitment among equals and sharp limitation of leadership powers, they regarded the prevailing forms of domination in Israel as irreligious, that is, contrary to the will of Israel's God. The consequences they foresaw were the ruination of the people and the collapse or overthrow of the institutions of national life. A clearer understanding of the prophetic mixture of religion and political economy can be gained if a closer look is given to some of the features of communitarian political economy and religion as they are expressed in older texts from the tribal period.

A very early text is the Song of Deborah in Judges 5, which expresses the exuberance of the Israelite tribes on the occasion of their victory over the chariot forces of Canaanite city-states in the plain of Jezreel, an event that occurred about 1100 B.C.E. The guerrilla fighters of Israel came down out of the hills of Galilee and Samaria and successfully overpowered the massed Canaanite chariotry, probably through a combination of surprise attack and a torrential rainstorm that immobilized the enemy's superior weaponry.

> "In the days of Shamgar, son of Anath,
>   in the days of Jael, caravans/campaigns [of the Canaanites] ceased
>   and travelers kept to the byways.
> The peasantry grew fat
>   In Israel, they grew fat on booty.[8]
> When you arose, oh Deborah,
>   when you arose, a mother in Israel! . . .
> "Tell of it, you who ride on tawny asses,
>   you who sit on rich carpets
>   and you who walk by the way.

> To the sound of musicians at the watering places,
>> there they repeat the triumphs of Yahweh,
>> the triumphs of his peasantry in Israel."
>>> (Judges 5:6–7; 10–11; trans. Gottwald)

A more stylized liturgical text in Deuteronomy 33 also celebrates some of these early victories of the insurgent Israelites over their more numerous and powerfully armed enemies:

> "Yahweh came from Sinai,
>> and dawned from Seir upon them;
>> he shown forth from Mount Paran.
> He came with the consecrated fighting forces,[9]
>> fire flashing from his right hand.
> Yes, he loved his people;
>> all those consecrated to him were in his hand;
> so they followed in your steps,
>> receiving direction from you,
> when Moses commanded us a law,
>> as a possession for the assembly of Jacob.
> Thus Yahweh became king in Jeshurun,[10]
>> when the heads of the people were gathered,
>> all the tribes of Israel together. . . .

> "There is none like God, O Jeshurun,
>> who rides through the heavens to your help,
>> and in his majesty through the skies.
> The enduring God is your dwelling place,
>> and underneath are the ever secure arms.
> And he thrust out the enemy before you,
>> and said 'Destroy!'
> So Israel dwelt in safety,
>> the fountain of Jacob alone,
> in a land of grain and wine;
>> yes, his heavens drop down dew.
> Happy are you, O Israel!
> Who is like you, a people saved by Yahweh,
>> the shield of your help,
>> and the sword of your triumph!
> Your enemies shall come fawning to you,
>> and you shall tread upon their high places."
>>> (Deuteronomy 33:2–5; 26–29; trans. Gottwald)

These early poems are shot through with martial and chauvinist rhetoric, but if it is seen in the context of political economy—as part of the struggle to build and defend a communitarian society—what comes to view is a bunch of rag-tagged farmers who, though of no account in previous history, had achieved something by combining forces under the aegis of their empowering deity. Their exuberance and boasting makes sense in the circumstances. There is no God like Yahweh and no people like Israel! The nobodies of the earth "speak up" about how one of the high gods has lifted up this "scum of the earth" and made an autonomous people out of them.

We have to grasp the social placement of this kind of language to hear what it means for a country like the United States of America when its Jewish and Christian citizens imagine this nation to be the equivalent of biblical Israel and begin drawing conclusions about God's blessings that follow from such an equation![11] Language from the lips of underdog, insurgent peasants, when put in the mouths of citizens of the dominant oppressive power in the world today, simply will not work in the way it did originally. This is what Israel's prophets already recognized when they told Israel's later ruling classes that they could not speak and act as if they had warrants from God when they were at the same time oppressing their own people and violating the norms of the communitarian law. Religious claims can be valued differently depending upon the particular political economy in which they are made and the power position of those making them.

In this connection, a brief look should be given to the context and setting of communitarian laws and practices traditionally attached to Moses and thus placed in the foundation period of ancient Israel.[12] A body of laws in Exodus 21–23, called the Covenant Code, probably dates from the northern kingdom of Israel about a century after David. Indications are, however, that these laws originated in the tribal period when Israel was trying to exclude relations of social and economic domination from its common life. One of these ancient instructions reads in this way: "If you lend money to any of my people who is poor, you shall not be to him as a creditor; you shall not exact interest from him" (Exod. 22:25). What sort of a "loan" is in view? Normally a financial grant would not be called a loan unless there were some interest attached to it to compensate the creditor. Likewise, it was customary in ancient tributary societies to charge interest on loans to tax-encumbered and famine-devastated peasants. The Bible does not tell us the actual size of the tax and interest burdens, but informed estimates suggest that anywhere from 75 to 90 percent of a cultivator's annual yield might be consumed in taxes and interest on loans.[13] In the face of this onerous economic practice, the Israelite law speaks emphatically: You Israelites may not exact tribute in that way. If you extend help to a brother in need, you may not charge anything for it because you are not permitted to make profit on the unavoidable suffering of others.

Furthermore, the same corpus of laws requires that Israel must practice equitable justice in deciding disputes among fellow Israelites. " 'You shall not pervert the justice due to your poor in his suit. Keep far from a false charge and do not slay the innocent and righteous, for I will not acquit the wicked. And you shall take no bribe, for a bribe blinds the officials and subverts the cause of those who are in the right' " (Exod. 23:6–8).

It is precisely laws of this sort that the prophets saw violated all around them. Bribes were being lavishly extended and greedily received, and crushing interest rates were applied to loans that culminated in forfeiture of land and debt servitude. It is clear that the prophets did not regard these infractions as the isolated acts of a few anti-social persons. They found, rather, that the law was being systematically and deliberately ignored by rulers, officials, and the newly affluent who had prospered under the conditions of monarchic "economic growth." In one way or another the political and social leaders justified this unbridled use of power to enrich and enhance themselves. Military adventurism and conspicuous consumption among the well-to-do had laid heavier conscription and tax burdens on the people. Debt foreclosures had concentrated land in the hands of profiteers. Once-productive land lay in neglect or had been devastated by war. Isaiah is typical of his radical prophetic colleagues when he blasts the leaders of Israel for plundering and destroying the people of Israel put in their charge:

> Yahweh has taken his place to contend,
>   he stands to judge his people.
> Yahweh enters into judgment

with the elders and the princes of his people.
"It is you who have devoured the vineyard,
the spoil of the poor is in your houses.
What do you mean by crushing my people,
by grinding the faces of the poor?" says the Lord God of
Hosts.

(Isaiah 3:13–15; trans. Gottwald)

From Isaiah's perspective, Yahweh's people are not just the elders and the princes who have been able to do whatever they can get away with in wronging others for their own advantage. Yahweh's people include the poor, and the deity wants to know what the leaders think they are doing in crushing and grinding their own citizenry so mercilessly. For it is these very leaders who have "devoured the vineyard" of Israel that Yahweh planted in the expectation of producing good grapes, but to no avail.[14] Numerous other examples could be given of prophetic indictments against the moral dereliction of Israel's leaders, together with their warnings of severe judgment to come. The examples given here should serve, however, to establish the communitarian measuring rod by which these prophets evaluated public life.

A question naturally arises about this heavily moralized social preaching, just as it is asked about the moral critics of our own capitalist economy. Were the prophets exaggerating, laying it on a little thick for effect? Were they perhaps "grinding axes," being envious or resentful of leaders with whom they had personal quarrels? Such doubts and reservations are raised today about those who question the supposed achievements of the capitalist success story. Such critics are often dismissed as disgruntled "prophets of doom." It is objected that nobody need be poor in our society. If people really want to advance economically, they can do so. If there are a few "glitches" in the economy here and there, they will be cleared up soon enough to reward everybody who honestly tries to get ahead. So, in biblical times as now, it was always possible to dismiss the prophets as troublesome cranks or dangerous charlatans.

In the last analysis, the only way to respond to what critics of society are saying is to make an independent judgment. There is no other court of appeals to adjudicate individual judgment. The "vindication of history" and the "judgment of God" may represent higher tribunals, but they take inordinate time to emerge, and even then they remain subject to dispute. For example, the prophetic announcements of public ruin and collapse did receive verification of a sort when the Israelite kingdoms fell. Even then, however, there were those who did not agree with the prophets' alleged reasons for catastrophe. Some thought that God had simply abandoned them without cause, or that the prophetic agitation had created social unrest and division that caused the public ruin.[15] The same range of contradictory explanations for historical reversals continues to show up: Is the United States weak abroad because it is a big bully among the nations or because it is not tough enough? Does our economy suffer because it is built on contradictory premises or because we have not given it free reign? It matters greatly with what eyes we see events and with what ears we hear contending voices. What do we read? To whom do we listen? What do we choose to see and what to ignore? When are the dark truths about our society and our culture too painful to look upon?

The political context of the prophets can be summed up as follows: The original impulse of Israel was to create a communitarian society that empowered the poor and denied to anyone the right to lord it over others. This impulse was sharply challenged and frustrated by Israel's own resort to kingship and also by her experience of exile and dispersion among the tributary world empires. During this long retreat from communitarian social practice, the prophets of Israel and Jesus himself upheld the neglected and violated communitarian norms and practices. The later history of Judaism and Christianity suggests that the synagogue and church have usually adapted to whatever political economy in which they were found, whether it was tributary, slave, feudal, capitalist, or socialist. On the other hand, courageous dissent and resistance to oppression and exploitation have been carried on by a significant minority of Jews and Christians, inspired and directed by the communitarian voices of the Bible and the liberative traditions of both religions.

How, then, might a biblical economic scheme be applied today? Does the Bible give a clear plan or model for economic life? Given the methodological difficulties already mentioned, any answer must remain personal.

The Bible does not give a plan or model of economics proper, but it does give something more valuable: a perspective and cri-

teria for evaluating political economies and a framework and
ground for accepting personal responsibility for one's economic
views and actions.[16] The "communitarian" yardstick is a significant one for assessing any political economy: Does that mode of
production, and the power relations governing it, build up the
whole community, providing it basic services and creating opportunities to realize the life possibilities of the greatest number of
people? If that is roughly the biblical measure of political economy, then I would conclude that the failures of socialist economies, while extensive and severe in many respects, are matched
and even exceeded by the failures of capitalist societies. This
"greater failure" of capitalism can be stated in various ways, but
one of the plainest ways to say it is this: The most powerful
capitalist nation in the world gains the advantage of wealth that it
has by "bleeding" and dominating smaller nations, the majority
of whose citizens live in deepening poverty, and at the same time
it allows a very large part of its own population to suffer in poverty. Public needs go begging, while a small part of the populace
lives in opulence and surfeit of goods. The political leadership is
almost totally captive to the ruling economic interests.

Does the Bible address the problem of developing a political
economy that serves the basic needs of all and does so by involv-
ing people in a process of self-government—not only politically,
but economically? No economic plan or model in the Bible can be
used because they are all pre-capitalist and pre-socialist, predat-
ing the state of the economic universe as it now exists. Small
groups of Jews or Christians can certainly develop communitarian
economic groupings, but political economy on a large scale must
be developed afresh.

In this regard, it may be that humane economics will have to
develop in the direction of democratic socialism, since capitalism
contains the fundamental flaw of selfish egoism at its very foundation. But the details of all this, and the specific mechanisms and
processes for working it out, are not to be found in the Bible as
prescriptions translatable into the contemporary situation. The
current task is to work them out along the lines of the communitarian impulse that runs in tandem with the Jewish and Christian
religions. To the degree that the communitarian impulse to equality and justice tempers the harsh features of unrestrained capitalism, it can be said that the resulting political economy is more

humanly fulfilling than capitalism (when allowed to run riot). Personally speaking, however, the capitalist structure is the wrong starting point for the economy because it begins from a crude self-seeking individualism that simply fails to serve the full range of human needs in community.[17]

What the Bible can do in a very powerful way is to sensitize persons to look across class lines to the world as people in different circumstances see it. Since most of the kind of analytic thinking represented in this essay is carried out by people in relatively advantaged positions, some help is needed to see the world as the poor and the disadvantaged see it.

Surprisingly, the voice of the poor and needy sounds throughout the Bible more persistently than in any other classical literature. The danger is that its stirring scenes and messages will be turned into an ancient morality play that no longer connects with our world. The truth is that the cruelty and neglect suffered by the poor and deprived of the earth continue in our time without any surcease and threaten the security and integrity of everyone in the process. On this point the Bible is as contemporary a document as can be imagined. Without giving specific instructions, it says again and again in stunning ways that something must be done about mass economic injustice in our world if this is to become God's earth and we are to be God's people.[18]

So, we are left with the logically perplexing but morally empowering paradox that the Bible is both grossly irrelevant in direct application to current economic problems and incredibly relevant in vision and principle for grasping opportunities and obligations to make the whole earth and its bounty serve the welfare of the whole human family. Such is the tantalizing economic legacy of biblical law and prophecy.

---

[1] Norman K. Gottwald, "Sociology of Ancient Israel," in *The Anchor Bible Dictionary* (Garden City: Doubleday, forthcoming). Also known as the Asiatic mode of production, tributary political economy is fully treated in A. M. Bailey and J. R. Llobera, *The Asiatic Mode of Production, Science, and Politics* (London: Routledge & Kegan Paul, 1981).

[2] The circumstances and details of Israel's emergence, viewed from the angles of political economy and religion, are developed voluminously in Norman K.

Gottwald, *The Tribes of Yahweh: A Sociology of the Religion of Liberated Israel, 1250–1050 B. C. E.* (Maryknoll, N.Y.: Orbis, 1979).

[3]The complicated issue of the development of Israelite and Jewish ethnic identity is examined in Norman K. Gottwald, "Religious Conversion and the Societal Origins of Ancient Israel," *Perspectives in Religious Studies* 15 (1988): 49–65.

[4]The way in which the exodus came to epitomize the social revolutionary building of community in early Israel is described in Norman K. Gottwald, "The Exodus as Event and Process: A Test Case in the Biblical Grounding of Liberation Theology," in *The Future of Liberation Theology: Essays in Honor of Gustavo Gutierrez*, ed. M. H. Ellis and O. Maduro (Maryknoll, N.Y.: Orbis, 1989), 250–260.

[5]The intertwining of conflicts over political economy and religion in the subsequent course of biblical history is presented in Norman K. Gottwald, *The Hebrew Bible: A Socio-Literary Introduction* (Philadelphia: Fortress Press, 1985).

[6]The implications of a proper political economic understanding for the work and teaching of Jesus are spelled out for biblical interpretation and preaching in Norman K. Gottwald, *Proclamation 4: Aids for Interpreting the Lessons of the Church Year, Series A: Pentecost 3* (Minneapolis: Augsburg-Fortress, 1989).

[7]For an understanding of the prophets in the context of communitarian norms and practices, see especially R. B. Coote, *Amos among the Prophets: Composition and Theology* (Philadelphia: Fortress, 1981), and W. J. Doorly, *Prophet of Justice: Understanding the Book of Amos* (New York: Paulist Press, 1989).

[8]This translation of Judges 5:7, in which Israel's peasantry is celebrated as "growing fat" on booty, has been proposed by Marvin L. Chaney of San Francisco Theological Seminary in his unpublished Ph.D. dissertation, Harvard University, 1976. Explanation of the grounds for this undoubtedly correct rendering are presented in Gottwald, *The Tribes of Yahweh*, 503–7.

[9]My translation of "consecrated fighting forces" as a double entendre on Israel's army and on supportive heavenly elements as an army is explained in Gottwald, *The Tribes of Yahweh*, 278–282.

[10]"Upright one," poetic term of endearment for Israel.

[11]For more on this equation of biblical Israel with the United States, see Norman K. Gottwald, "Are Biblical and U.S. Societies Comparable?" *Radical Religion* 3/1 (1976): 17–24.

[12]On some of the sociological dimensions and implications of the Covenant Code in Exodus 21–23, see E. von Waldow, "Social Responsibility and Social Structure in Early Israel," *Catholic Biblical Quarterly* 32 (1970): 182–204.

[13]D. E. Oakman, *Jesus and the Economic Question of His Day* (Lewiston: The Edwin Mellen Press, 1986), 57–80.

[14]See, for instance, the Son of the Vineyard in Isaiah 5:1–8. On the importance of Isaiah 3:13–15, and for a proper interpretation of the Song of the Vineyard, see G. T. Sheppard, "The Anti-Assyrian Redaction and the Canonical Context of Isaiah 1–39," *Journal of Biblical Literature* 104 (1985): 193–216.

[15]That the radical prophets and other reformist elements in ancient Israel, including the Deuteronomists, were actually the cause of the downfall of the

Israelite kingdoms has been argued by M. Silver, *Prophets and Markets: The Political Economy of Ancient Israel* (Boston: Kluwer-Nijhoff, 1983). In my judgment, Silver is able to reach this conclusion only by ignoring taxation and debt burdens within Israel and the balance of power among ancient Near East states.

[16]J. L. Segundo, *Liberation Theology* (Maryknoll, N. Y.: Orbis, 1976), 97–124, articulates this point by means of a distinction between "faith" as the commitment to liberation and "ideologies" as political analyses and actions pertinent to particular historical situations. The Bible is rich in ideologies, and familiarity with them inspires us, not to try to copy one or another of them— which we cannot do in any case—but to seek out the necessary ideology for our situation in order to fill "the empty space between the conception of God that we receive from our faith and the problems that come to us from an ever-changing history."

[17]More extensive ethical assessments of the theory and practice of capitalism and socialism are set forth in Norman K. Gottwald, "From Biblical Economics to Modern Economics: A Bridge over Troubled Waters," *Churches in Struggle: Liberation Theologies and Social Change in North America*, ed. W. K. Tabb (New York: Monthly Review Press, 1986), 138–148, and "Values and Economic Structures," *Religion, the Economy, and Social Justice*, ed. M. Zweig (New York: Cambridge University Press, forthcoming).

[18]M. D. Meeks, *God the Economist: The Doctrine of God and Political Economy* (Minneapolis: Fortress, 1989), pursues the provocative and original theological method of examining what economic assumptions and behaviors are most in accord with God conceived under the metaphor of "the economist," i.e., as "householder" or "manager" of creation, society, and church. Among works on the biblical grounding of liberation theologies, the one that makes most sophisticated and trenchant use of political economy, ancient and modern, is I. J. Mosala, *Biblical Hermeneutics and Black Theology in South Africa* (Grand Rapids: Eerdmans, 1989).

CHAPTER 2

The Prophetic Tradition, Economic Efficiency, and the Quest for Justice

William K. Tabb
Professor of Economics
Queens College, CUNY

Irving Kristol, on the occasion of a public lecture, identified himself as a neoorthodox Jew of the non-practicing persuasion and explained that the terms "prophetic" and "rabbinic" indicate the two poles within which the Jewish tradition operates. "They are not equal poles," Kristol said. "The rabbinic is the stronger pole, always." In an Orthodox Hebrew school, he went on, "the prophets are read only by those who are far advanced. . . . The prophets are only for people who are advanced in their learning, and not likely to be misled by prophetic fervor."[1]

Leaving aside any pedagogic issues of precedence, Kristol seems to be saying that the rabbinical tradition, having authority on its side, has marginalized the prophetic tradition—in effect locked up the prophetic writings—and has allowed them to be read only by those who have been properly inoculated by status quo realism. One is permitted to read the prophets when one is less likely to be too swayed by them. (It was not that way, however, when I studied at Stephen Wise Free Synagogue.)

What, then, have the prophets to do with economic life? Abraham Heschel in his study *The Prophets* claims that "the prophet was an individual who said No to his society, condemning its habits and assumptions, its complacency, waywardness and syncretism. He was often compelled to proclaim the very opposite of what his heart expected. His fundamental objective was to reconcile man and God. . . . Why do the two need reconciliation?" Heschel asked. "Perhaps it is due to man's false sense of sovereignty, to his abuse of freedom, to his aggressive, sprawling pride, resenting God's involvement in history."[2]

Like the prophets, liberation theologians welcome God's involvement in history. They cherish God's covenant with people of faith. And again, like the prophets, liberation theologians' deep sensitivity to evil can be called hysterical. There are some who want the young to be protected from the fiery pronouncements of these disturbing figures of contemporary theology. But if their sensitivities, like the biblical prophets, are "to be called hysterical, what name should be given to the abysmal indifference to evil which the prophet bewails?"[3]

The prophetic tradition is troublesome. After thousands of years the pages of the Bible still seem to burn with indignation. One can understand the consternation prophets cause to temple authorities who see their job as representing the status quo. They read the Bible for a sense of order and instead are thrown into

> orations about widows and orphans, about the corruption of judges and affairs of the market place. Instead of showing us a way through the elegant mansions of the mind, the prophets take us to the slums. The world is a proud place, full of beauty, but the prophets are scandalized, and rave as if the whole world were a slum. They make much ado about things, lavishing excessive language upon trifling subjects. . . . The things that horrify the prophets are even now daily occurrences all over the world.[4]

Thus speaks Abraham Heschel.

No "Rambo" could consent to the reign of a God who would call the archenemy of God's people, Assyria, the "rod of my anger" (Isa. 10:5), who could call Nebuchadrezzar, the king of Babylon, "my servant" whom God promised to "bring . . . against this land and its inhabitants" (Jer. 25:9). Why does this God not rather criticize the Assyrians? In a fair comparison, is Israel not the best society there has ever been? What an unpatriotic God this God of Israel could be!

This prophetic understanding of Judaism is arguably more faithful to the heritage than the version offered by Irving Kristol. Perhaps the most familiar pronouncement of the prophet Amos was also spoken powerfully in Martin Luther King's southern cadence at that great gathering in Washington in 1964:

> Even though you offer me your burnt offerings and cereal
>   offerings,
>   I will not accept them,
> and the peace offerings of your fatted beasts
>   I will not look upon.
> Take away from me the noise of your songs;
>   to the melody of your harps I will not listen.
> But let justice roll down like waters,
>   and righteousness like an ever-flowing stream.
>
> (Amos 5:22–24)

The prophetic motif remains fully within the rabbinical tradition.

The contrast between those who maintain the prophetic rabbinical tradition and those who do not is duplicated among those doing theology from a Christian perspective. In a review in *Christianity and Crisis*, Robert McAfee Brown contrasts the way Michael Novak interprets the Christian doctrine of the incarnation to a liberation theology perspective:

> Novak does not affirm that because "the Word was made flesh and dwelt among us" new possibilities exist on the human scene that free us to lead daring, even risky, lives. Instead, he claims that "The point of Incarnation is to respect the world as it is, to acknowledge its limits, to recognize its weaknesses, irrationalities and evil forces, and to disbelieve any promise that the world is now or ever will be transformed into the Kingdom of God." What this provides, whether Novak so intends it or not, is a splendid theological justification for the status quo, for complacent acceptance of things as they are, since it is not only unrealistic, but even un-Christian, to believe we can change things. Conclusion: *"The Incarnation obliges us to reduce our noblest expec-*

tations." Surely the Christian faith proclaims the opposite: The Incarnation obliges us to enlarge our noblest expectations, since by virtue of God's presence in the world we know that we are not alone, that God will empower us in challenging evil in the world, and that the vision of the Kingdom of God (which Jesus assured us was already "in our midst") acts as a prod, a stimulus, and an enabler against complacency in the face of injustice. The Good News is that God wills liberation from bondage, not acceptance of it.[5]

One must note the ahistoricism, or what might be termed the false historicism, of the neoconservatives. Their method is that of comparative statics. In a sense, they assume a position antithetical to the prophets, who are in pain, a pain caused by the injustice of their own society. The prophets burn to make it better. They call a fallen community and each of its members to return to faithfulness. The prophetic tradition is one that does not apologize for an unjust status quo, but calls for a renewed commitment to "love mercy, do justice and walk humbly with God" in this world.

The neoconservative theologians are uncomfortable with the prophetic tradition. Their method is different. The point of much neoconservative thinking is to celebrate America—partly for the wrong reasons. They attempt to ward off prophetic criticism by tarring critics with guilt by association. Thus they confuse anger at injustice either with being soft on communism or with being naive about what is possible.[6]

The picture to be drawn here of current global economic trends and the class relations they embody is not pleasant. The effects of the forces at work are to play nation against nation, increase insecurity, and bypass the issues of growing poverty and inequality. The point of calling attention to depressing trends and the need for change is not to be negative and defeatist, however. If a prophetic agenda is to be pursued under contemporary circumstances, it must be remembered with Rabbi Heschel that

> It is not a world devoid of meaning that evokes the prophet's consternation, but a world deaf to meaning. And yet the consternation is but a prelude. He always begins with a message of doom and concludes with a message of hope and redemption.[7]

This call to a new form of hope seems to be precisely why neoconservatives—more than others—are so uncomfortable with

the prophetic tradition. They close their ears to the type of redemption the prophets earnestly urge on humanity. The prophets
claim that God enjoins people to do justice here and now, to
return to faithfulness. In response to that claim, Christians and
Jews need to develop not only a critique of present political economic realities but an agenda of faithfulness. That this must be
done in reference to the Novaks and Kristols is only because
Reaganism yet governs America during the administration of
George Bush.

In the 1960s and even more so in the 1930s the central ideas
now labeled "neoconservative" were even more powerfully argued than they are today, as evidenced by the frequent citations
of von Mises, von Hayek, Friedman, and Goldwater in current
neoconservative writings. That George Gilder is believed to have
more to say on the causes of poverty than Michael Harrington is
a depressing sign of the times. It is not, however, a measure of the
relative merits of their arguments. It is, rather, one result of a
different constellation of power dynamics. Thus, while there may
be some merit in debating the validity and usefulness of neoconservative analysis as a guide to policy, it is more important to
ask why the times have changed. And it is also important to
consider how the larger constraining context in which intellectual
questions are asked is likely to develop. What change seems realistic is in part a question of how we understand what *is*.

Capital accumulation patterns always have differential impacts on class formation. For instance, if our economy creates
fewer good middle-class jobs and more poverty-level ones (along
with a relative growth in the number of the very rich), that is
going to have impact on our social structures and political institutions. In this light, this essay will explore an analysis of the
current status of capitalism in the United States within a historical
perspective, an estimate of the current trends, and some sugges-
tions of how people in a prophetic tradition might reflect on this
situation.

Over the last decade or two, disturbing questions have been
raised about the long-cherished assumptions of upward mobility
and unlimited growth—essential elements of the American
dream. The middle class (the upper end of the working class) has
taken a buffeting in the last two decades. The evidence for this is
summarized in the data showing that the income of the average

worker today in real purchasing power is what it was in 1973. Why? What happened in the American economy? An answer requires some historical perspective.

At the end of the Second World War, the blue-collar industrial unions made an unwritten but understood arrangement with industry that they would stop organizing the unorganized, agree to the corporations' control of technology, not form a labor party, and support the bipartisan foreign policy of the Cold War. In exchange the corporations said: "We will keep giving you good pay, keeping up with productivity and then some. If you are in the privileged sector, the primary labor market, you will do just fine. But the price of this is that you must not organize the rest of the unemployed. But see what a good deal it is? The unemployed will get less; you will get more." American labor accepted that. They accepted it in part because the trade-union movement at the end of the Second World War had changed dramatically. The militancy of the 1930s and 1940s was replaced with the business unionism of the 1950s. This change was fostered by the government and the corporations who claimed, with some justification, that there were many communists in the unions.[8] Anyone who was militant, who said that employment security and job safety were important, was considered a "communist." In the Cold War climate of the 1950s, many of the people who put the *movement* into the labor movement were forced out of the unions. The new labor leaders thought like company executives, and some paid themselves like their peers in the corporate world.[9]

Without adequate militancy and grass roots participation, unions were unprepared to respond in the period from 1965 to the present when their relative privilege was eroded as capital became internationalized. Now, the steel mills in Brazil and South Korea are able to supply not only the world market but the United States market as well. American corporations make their new investments outside of the United States and are an important element of the foreign competition. This means that the unions, which once grew strong by remaining in isolation from their sisters and brothers around the world, have undercut their own position. Now, since these unions do not understand solidarity, and they submit to a South Korea that forbids unions to organize, the Koreans—supported by up-to-date technology and United States financing—undersell American-made goods. Conditions in

South Korea are what they were in the beginning of the twentieth century in the United States. Solidarity is in the interest of United States workers in the narrow sense that a pattern of South Korean development stressing increasing local living standards would help workers both here and there. Within the current policy, reflecting a low-wage export strategy, the American living standard is driven down. From 1979 to 1985 in the United States, poverty rose 23 percent in female-headed families and 32 percent in married-couple families. Poverty rates have returned to what they were before the War on Poverty in 1965. A study released by the Joint Economic Committee of Congress shows that since 1979, all of the net growth in employment has occurred in jobs earning under $14,000 a year.[10] Three-fifths of these jobs paid under $7,000 a year.

These statistics indicate that more and more of the new poor are working people. There are people who are working in McDonald's who would like to have families of their own, who would like to have a home of their own, but are living with their parents. They cannot afford rent for an apartment. They may never be able to buy a house. The cost of housing relative to income is pricing this generation out of home ownership.

The jobs that are growing are in the service sector.[11] Overwhelmingly, the jobs that are growing the fastest are retail, trade, health, and business services. These now constitute half of total private employment. They pay poverty-zone wages. What this represents is growth in service-sector jobs that offer a low living standard, no union protection, and no health benefits. Many of these jobs are part-time. As Americans get older and government services are cut, many are moving toward a Third World standard of living. Their standard of living is well above the Third World level today, but the trend is downward, as is usually the case in periods of crisis and overcapacity.

It appears to this essayist and other economists that what is happening is a period of global restructuring, a long-term crisis, a slow 1929. Writing from the vantage point of the 1930s, Maurice Dobb noted that even with a lot of workers unemployed, labor power was not being cheapened fast enough to suit capital. Many economists wanted the governments of the advanced capitalist nations to help force wages down. The effect of such pressures was to create a class-based political movement.

We are confronted with this significant difference between the position today and in the classic days of the early and mid-nineteenth century: namely, that insofar as labour has developed today strong defensive organizations capable of resistance, the old classic law of the "industrial reserve army" fails to operate unaided. This, indeed, is the crux of the complaint of economists since 1920, when they have spoken of the need to introduce "flexibility and plasticity" into the limbs of the economic system, and in particular into the labour market. Today, recourse to this device requires extraordinary measures— extraordinary measures to break this resistance of which nineteenth century liberalism scarcely dreamed.[12]

These measures failed and instead a progressive backlash developed.

There are others who share this view of the 1930s. Samuel Lubell, the eminent political scientist who conducted in-depth voter interviews, concluded that support for the New Deal indicated "a class conscious vote for the first time in American history. The New Deal appears to have accomplished what the Socialists, the IWW, and the Communists never could approach. It has drawn a class line across the face of American politics." A poll taken in 1942, for example, showed that 25 percent of the respondents agreed that "some form of socialism would be a good thing . . . for the country as a whole." Possibly more people supported socialism in the 1930s. We do not know because it took Roper until 1942 to ask, and no other survey conducted in the 1930s asked explicitly about socialism. The polls of that decade did show a majority in favor of public ownership of utilities with a good number (41 percent in 1937) favoring government ownership of banks. Moreover, opinion was stratified by class. Workers favored government ownership and redistribution programs. The well-to-do did not.

These attitudes fade in the American Century—that twenty-year period following the end of the Second World War—and a mood of antipathy toward government ownership is evident to the present. People react positively to free enterprise, although they are likely to condemn particular corporate abuses. They also condemn big government but support specific welfare programs.

As the American Century of generalized upward mobility wanes, there are efforts to restore laissez-faire policies and politics. These efforts to return to the 1920s have their dangers, and it is of more than passing interest that while Ronald Reagan frequently invoked FDR, it was a portrait of Calvin Coolidge he chose to adorn the walls of the cabinet room. The shape of the Reagan years may some day look very different from what they do to those who today are still caught up with Reagan as the "Great Communicator." Roosevelt said in 1939:

> For twelve years this nation was afflicted while hear-nothing, see-nothing government looked away. Nine mocking years with the golden calf and three long years of the scourge! Nine crazy years at the ticker and three long years in the breadlines! Nine mad years of mirage and three long years of despair! Powerful influences strive today to restore that kind of government with its doctrine that the government is best which is most indifferent.

If Ronald Reagan and George Bush do not represent the end of the policies we identify with Reaganomics, and if another Great Depression will not necessarily occur tomorrow, there is yet some resonance in Sidney Blumenthal's question, "If Reagan Is Not Roosevelt, but Coolidge, Who Will Be Hoover?"[13]

One need not predict another Great Depression, a crisis that looks like an exact replay of that era (although there are too many disquieting parallels not to take this threat as a possibility). What appears to be happening, rather, is a transformational crisis, a painful restructuring which—unless it is brought under conscious social control—will mean hard times, exploitation, and alienation for most Americans.

One learns from Michael Novak's *The Spirit of Democratic Capitalism* that contemporary capitalism is better than both precapitalist feudalism and Soviet communism. The interesting comparisons, however, are between the United States and the other advanced capitalist nations, especially the strong social democratic welfare states. There is no instruction from Novak about how to make American society better because on this most important question the neoconservatives are quiet. Novak thinks "democratic capitalism" is pretty good and its workings should not be disturbed.[14] Yet, changes *are* happening, and the questions are really whether they are good changes and whether better changes can be made.

A more useful book for addressing these questions is Goren Therborn's *Why Some Peoples Are More Unemployed Than Others: The Strange Paradox of Growth and Unemployment*. Therborn argues that there are viable full-employment strategies, that the same global crisis causes more unemployment in some nations than in others, and that it is possible to discern which options have made more sense from a working class point of view. Drawing on his findings, consideration can be given to the domestic situation in the United States.

The conventional excuses for high unemployment—women in the labor force, the entry of baby boomers, and so on—do not prove robust when tested in the light of cross-national data. In order to absorb new labor supply, some nations have followed policies that are objectively better than those followed in other countries. Policy choice is the key. Five countries have done the best over the decade 1974 to 1984. On the surface they would seem to be a diverse lot: Austria, Norway, Switzerland, Sweden, and Japan. The countries that have done worst also seem disparate: Belgium, the Netherlands, Britain, Canada, and Denmark. The United States is in the medium-high unemployment group, along with France, Germany, Australia, and Finland.

On the question of the welfare state, strong welfare states should be distinguished from soft welfare states. The one strong welfare state is Sweden, with generous social commitments, a relatively developed public control of the economy, and a successful institutionalized commitment to full employment. The soft welfare states, Belgium, Denmark, and the Netherlands, which also have extensive social policies, have little control of their economies and show little concern or success with unemployment. They simply pay benefits to the unemployed. There are also two full-employment nations with very underdeveloped welfare states: Switzerland and Japan.

There are many other interesting comparisons. Sweden has the highest standard of living, the highest rate of part-time work, and the lowest number of actual hours worked by industrial workers. Youth unemployment is highest in Italy and France. High unemployment may mean massive suffering, as in the punitive industrial crisis in Thatcher's England, or a better deal, as in the compensated general-crisis unemployment of the welfare state of the Netherlands. In both Italy and Belgium, unemployment falls disproportionately on youth and women. In Belgium, it is compensated; in Italy, it is not.

Because citizens of the United States tend to think about their country in isolation from the rest of the world, such social and economic differences as those between Denmark and Belgium are confusing to many.

Academic social policy often presents socialist England as a failure that Thatcher is trying to retrieve. But England has a terrible welfare state and, as Therborn suggests, hardly merits the label. Americans are told that wages must go down in the United States if this country is to compete internationally, but Japanese and European experience shows this not necessarily to be true.

Therborn finds the existence of an institutionalized commitment to full employment to be the basic explanation for the differential impact of the current crisis. Such a policy stance involves an explicit commitment to achieving and maintaining full employment, the existence of counter-cyclical policies, including specific mechanisms to fit potential workers with jobs in the economy, and a conscious decision not to use high unemployment to secure some other policy end. Full employment cannot be reached if it is decided—as has been done in the Reagan and Thatcher administrations—that cutting inflation is a more important goal, and that it is best achieved by generating unemployment to force wages and the working class standard of living down.

The countries that have full-employment policies do so either because a politically dominant labor movement has forced such policies or, ironically, because of a conservative concern with order and stability, which are considered to be important to capital accumulation (as in Japan and Switzerland). Neither of these latter countries is a welfare state, but neither accepts free-market dogma. State-backed cartels and planning are historic features of both nations.

The countries that have done worst in terms of employment over this 1974–1984 period are those that have most applied restrictive monetarism. They are Belgium, the Netherlands, and the United Kingdom. And full-employment countries all pursued expansive Keynesian sorts of policies. Even for Japan, Therborn finds domestic stimulation to have been more important than the export sector for growth. But Keynesianism was not enough. Some nations failed using Keynesian policies. Successful Keyne-

sianism required consistently complementary monetary policy
—in particular, a low-interest-rate policy. Success also was related
to specific and direct intervention in the market. It was such a
combination of policies that worked for Sweden, Norway, Japan,
Austria, and Switzerland.

Sweden is the exemplar of what active labor-market policies
can achieve. Its theory is to force inefficient low-wage businesses
to upgrade so that they provide better jobs at higher pay or go out
of business. At the same time, it follows expansionary Keynesian
policies for growth and public vocational (re)training programs.
Unlike such programs in the United States, training programs in
Sweden are high quality and are directed toward jobs that actually
exist. In 1984, 70 percent of such trainees were employed after six
months.

The Japanese expand public investment, a much higher pro-
portion of that nation's total investment, in fact, than most capitalist nations. A major part of the full-employment policy is the
intra-firm mobility of workers promised lifetime employment,
even if their conglomerate owner moves them from textiles or
shipbuilding to electronics or services jobs.

Without considering the particulars of each country, the generalization that emerges from Therborn's work is that significant
control of one or more strategic economic variables on the market
can, and has been, used to provide full employment. The Swiss,
for instance, throw out foreign workers, reducing supply to create
full employment; the Austrians provide inexpensive credit for
private investment and expand public sector activity. The point is
that active intervention can work well.

These success stories are not protectionist. The activist policies they follow are consistent with vigorous participation in
world capitalist markets but on terms set in part by national policies and priorities.

Changes in manufacturing, Therborn finds, have had virtually no bearing on international differences in the rise of unemployment across advanced capitalist nations. Japan continues a
relatively high level of manufacturing employment but changes
its composition dramatically to adjust to changes in the work and
acts to generate alternative employment. Neither is easy, but their
institutions committed to full employment have worked relatively
well. Of course, all of these countries are in economic trouble too,

even Japan. But it is also interesting that each of the relatively successful nations does *not* play by the rules of the game. That is, none is a member of the European Community and so is free to follow nationalistic policies, and none of these economies has been deeply penetrated by foreign enterprises. They maintain autonomy and put national full employment ahead of other policies. This is not to say that they are unsuccessful in international competition. Not only does Japan do well under the hegemony of capital, but Swedish multinationals, like Electrolux and Volvo, do well with strong unions, high taxes, and an intrusive state pursuing social security and full employment. The expectation and reality of social stability means interest groups are more willing to cooperate honestly despite differing interests.

Clearly this is the opposite of the "lean and mean" model followed by the United States and Britain. It is also different from the versions of the welfare state that leave private capital to run the productive sector but pay good benefits to those who cannot find jobs. There is no clear evidence that the latter nations create a welfare dependency by their unemployment (and other) benefits. These nations can, however, be contrasted to the various full-employment models already discussed. Again, the compensating high-unemployment regimes stand in contrast to primitive high-unemployment regimes.

Most significant in Therborn's central theme is the understanding that contemporary society is not undergoing a technological revolution that inexorably creates mass unemployment. The same worldwide crisis has differential results depending on what nations choose to do in terms of public policy. Variations in contemporary unemployment are due mainly to specific national systems of political economy and not to universal market relationships, as most economists and the Reagan administration contended.

Therborn prefers to describe as "pressures" those things that economists call the "causes" of high unemployment—for example, the growth of female labor-force participation and the loss of demand for particular products. Also, in considering what can and cannot be done in the United States because of the way its economic system works, Therborn suggests that such constraints not be accepted as "given." They are, rather, largely defined politically and ideologically by long-standing power relationships now internalized as norms and expectations. They can be transcended. Therborn's conclusions are in a profound sense optimistic ones.

Mass unemployment is not a necessary effect of anonymous and evil forces of contemporary capitalism—it is an inherent potentiality of capitalism. And it could have been controlled had support been withdrawn from right-wing politicians and economic advisers, from faint-hearted or weak-willed Social Democrats, and, sometimes, from starry-eyed trade unionists who credulously accepted liberal arguments. And, significantly, it has been controlled in five of sixteen countries under review.[15]

Interestingly, like Barnett and Müller in *Global Reach*[16] over a decade ago, Therborn speaks of one possible future as the "Brazilianization" of advanced capitalism. Brazilianization will be characterized by mass unemployment, increasing income inequality, and a trichotomous socio-economic division. At the bottom will be the permanently and marginally unemployable. In the middle will be those making an acceptable living and glad not to be in the bottom group. And finally, those on top, the managers, will be better paid and connected to command and management positions. It appears that New York City already looks like this.

Therborn also offers a possible scenario for a labor comeback. It is easier to stipulate the economic policies it would require than the political strategy for its realization. The economics of national full employment would require institutional changes reflating the economy through investment in real plant and equipment and away from speculative paper entrepreneurship. Active labor markets would need a revolution in educational policy to reverse the present trend in an America that is becoming illiterate and unable to solve coherently its intellectual problems. This revolution would encompass vocational training, public works, part-time jobs with benefits, and a willingness of labor to accommodate to new technologies, in exchange for which employment guarantees would be written in stone. Further, there would need to be policies for equal-employment opportunity for racial minorities and women, and concern for the environment.

The growth in the numbers of poor and homeless in America, the decline in education and health—these are the results of misguided economic policies—policies that should be denounced on prophetic grounds, but also as a matter of a more sensible economics. The quest for justice, to reward adequately the workers and to help those in need, makes economic sense. In Germany and Japan, two major economic competitors of the United States, investing in people is an integral part of successful national economic policies.

Therborn may well be unduly optimistic about the abilities of any one nation to escape the pressures of the internationalization process, even if that nation pursues the policies he says have been successful. Until there are commonly formed and accepted international policies imposed to some degree on all economies, economic fragility and downward pressures on wages and working and living conditions will persist. Nevertheless, since economic policy does matter, the United States could do much better than it presently does.

Therborn's analysis deserves the attention it has received here because it has much to teach about progressive class politics. A new national agenda in this country depends upon enough pressure being exerted from the grass roots. There does seem to be a growing movement for economic justice in this nation, and it can have a real impact. If the moral issues can be clarified, others will come forward to be political leaders at the appropriate time.

In trying to dismantle the welfare state, neoconservatives focus on the alleged dependence created by government handouts. They also reject the liberal contention that there should be decent jobs and adequate pay, along with training, education, and other requisites for people to do these jobs well. Instead, all individuals are considered to be complete on their own, with whatever resources they and their families can bring to the struggle for existence. It is important, say the neoconservatives, to do away with subsistence social programs.

Frances Fox Piven and Richard Cloward write from a different perspective. "Employers have always understood that subsistence resources interfere with wage labor. Indeed, labor markets did not become widespread in the first place until most of the subsistence resources of the pre-industrial community had been eliminated."[17] Indeed, the violence required to create the new class society of capitalism in which some had a monopoly on the means of production and others had nothing to sell but their labor power is more accurately portrayed by Marx than by Novak. That private charity plays less a role than the state in meeting basic needs in a class society is secondary to the meliorating and system-preserving aspect of redistribution. But central to the concern with economic justice is Piven and Cloward's conclusion that "what has flared up in our time is nothing less than the recurring conflict between property rights and subsistence rights, which originated with the emergence of capitalism itself."[18] The new class war—or the intensification of the conflict—comes from efforts by an ascendent capital to impose new terms on working people. It is the theme of Piven and Cloward's work that in our times we see the struggle to reestablish the unity of the economic and political spheres, the separation of which Novak celebrates.

The remarkable achievement of capitalism, Novak, Piven, and Cloward would agree, was the radical departure from the experiences and ideas of the pre-industrial community, in which economic and political roles had been fused. For Novak, this is the genius of the new order; to Piven and Cloward it is its major fault. The world of the market is in effect shielded from the world of politics to which common people had gained access.

The Great Depression and the New Deal changed this. The form of the corporate state in the period after the Second World War is the welfare state. If General Motors, General Electric, and the other generals of United States capitalism profit from the federal highway program and FHA- and VA-financed suburbanization, so too do millions of American working people who enjoy refrigerators and washers, new homes and automobiles. The welfare state was, for most Americans, a positive development.

With the new internationalization of labor and capital, the United States becomes just one profit center that has to compete with others on increasingly less favorable terms. This explains why the neoconservative ideology has been so welcome in the halls of power. Separating the economic from the political is key to their dominance. To progressives, the best protection people have is still through the political process. The task is to make government responsive to the people rather than to the corporate elites.

When people became active in making history in this century (that is, in the 1930s and 1960s in America), politics and economics were fused. Political rights were used to address economic problems. Under such conditions, the state became the locus of class struggle. Piven and Cloward, in a series of important books, have demonstrated that

> Democracy finally offered people some defense against the historic alliance of state and capital—some protection against strike breaking, against the hazards of the workplace, against discrimination by race and sex, and against the unemployment and destruction that had always made people desperate enough to take any job on any terms.[19]

The degree of inequality in Western democracies in fact is found to vary inversely with the percentage of socialists who had been elected to the country legislature since 1945. The greater the socialist presence, the greater the amount of income that went to the lower classes.[20]

The limits of the acceptable political spectrum in the United States make even talking about these issues difficult.[21] For most of us, the period of affluence after the Second World War (1946 to 1966, or perhaps to 1973) is the norm out of which we build our political and economic expectations. But if American exceptionalism is coming to an end, we may come to view our freedom to choose the structures of our common life in a new light.

These developments also suggest why Keynesian and Marxist analysis will yet have another round of relevance to large numbers of social scientists. Keynes surfaces in the Brandt Report. It argues against continuing a war of each against all in which the nation-states compete to lower the standard of living of their citizens and the expenditures devoted to their collective life. It favors a collaborative effort simultaneously to increase wages and social spending to create markets, reduce unemployment, and restart the global growth engines. Rather than recommending Reagan-Thatcher styles of austerity, the Brandt Report argues that the world would be better off with global Keynesianism. If collective action were possible, this, the Keynesians say, would restore prosperity.

The magic of the marketplace, however, does not excite the hungry masses of the Third World, to whom the lure of the national liberty of democratic capitalism and the formal freedoms of market exchange conceal the substantive realms of suppression and exploitation. Third-World attraction to Marxism is of long standing. But in the leading capitalist nations the intensification of class struggle takes on new salience with the passing of generalized upward mobility and the realization, so central in Marx, that in spite of its historically progressive beginning, capitalism is an unsustainable mode of production.

Of interest also is to see who is raising issues of class-based politics in America today. During the last presidential election, a short article bore the headline: "Jackson Condemns 'Economic Violence' as He Opens Headquarters in Iowa." The idea of economic violence belongs to a class analysis. That a black American church person was reintroducing such thinking to our political discourse is interesting. When Mario Cuomo decided not to seek the presidential nomination, there were discussions concerning which other candidates would be helped most by the withdrawal of the most liberal of the potential front runners. Jesse Jackson was mentioned in these stories only briefly and dismissed as "the black candidate" without a chance of winning. Gary Hart (who apparently had less support among black and Hispanic voters than Jackson had among whites) was not described as "the white candidate." The implicit racism and the lack of serious attention given to Jackson's discussion of issues is troubling. Yet he was the only candidate who discussed issues in the context of a traditional Democratic Party discourse. For example, in Iowa he said:

> "When the stock market hits new records but manufacturing jobs hit new lows, when corporate profits keep climbing yet job salaries are plunging, when it is safer and more profitable in this country to sell Mercedes-Benz sedans than John Deere tractors, then it is time to get America, Inc., back on the track."

The tone struck by Jackson's political discourse can be contrasted with the advice of both party centrists and even liberals who urged the advocacy of even progressive programs in the language and rationales of lean and tough-minded realism.[22] Yet what needs to be discussed are the causes and implications of the shifts in income and wealth, industrial competitiveness, and sectional balance.

There is no easy translation of a prophetic faith into a political agenda, much less into support for a particular candidate or political philosophy. There should be suspicion of anyone—right, left, or center—who presumes to speak for God. Still, if religion is to have meaning in the lives of women and men, it has to affect who they are as social beings.

Drawing on analyses by Goren Therborn, Frances Fox Piven, Richard Cloward, and others, the suggestion has been made that class analysis has become increasingly relevant to understanding politics in the United States. In his book, *The New Politics of Inequality*, Washington Post political analyst Thomas Edsall does a brilliant job of discussing in class terms recent voting patterns and control of political agendas. One of the problems he articulates from the point of view of the democratic process is that the corporate rich have been able to buy politicians of both major parties to an increasing extent. This effectively disenfranchises the majority of voters who are unable to express their preferences because of a lack of viably funded alternative candidates.

The world described here is characterized by the economic trend of the internationalization of labor and capital, downward pressure on wages and living and working conditions, and a politics of implicit class polarization. Real issues are obscured, and racial, ethnic, regional, and religious differences accentuated. How, in this situation, are Jews and Christians to live out a faith commitment in the prophetic tradition?

From the perspective of a prophetic world view and witness, some elements of an agenda to be urged on the political process may be developed. But, prior to any political debate, there must be a wrestling with what it means to be in the prophetic tradition.

One such inquiry and statement, *Paths in Utopia*, which Martin Buber completed in 1945, offers a concluding thought in this direction. To Buber, the prophetic is a form of eschatology "which at any given moment sees every person addressed by it as endowed, in a degree not to be determined beforehand, with the power to participate by his decisions and deeds in the preparing of Redemption."[23] The second form of eschatology Buber discusses, the apocalyptic, he identifies with both ancient Persia and Marxism. Elements of the religious right are also apocalyptic. To them, as to some Marxists, the redemptive process in all its details—its very hour and course—has been fixed from everlasting. For the religious right, human beings are only tools of this redemptive process, although what is immutably fixed may yet be "unveiled" to them, and they may be assigned their function.

While Buber claims the mantle of "utopian" for himself, he is critical of the Soviets as being utopian in the sense criticized by Marx. The utopians that Marx critiqued (those that seem to form the core of the Soviet model that people like Novak condemn) urge what Buber calls "social architecture," a practice in which experts impose mechanistic solutions for all social problems. According to the Soviet model, human beings would be different in revolutionary, communist society. Not only has this proven not to be the case so far in societies calling themselves communist, the current unrest throughout the communist world points to its positive falsity. Yet coercion has continued. The state has not withered away, and a repressive apparatus has imposed a cost in human freedom and in productivity in narrow economic terms. This is the heart of Novak's critique and is a theme Gorbachev has sounded. Buber, the socialist, criticizes the Soviets in the name of his prophetic vision. The spontaneity and creativity that Novak believes can come only from capitalism are to be better developed, Buber suggests, in abolishing capitalism.

The fullest development of individuality, Kropotkin wrote, "will combine with the highest development of voluntary association in all its aspects, in all possible degrees and for all possible purposes; an association that is always changing, that bears in itself the elements of its own duration, that takes on the forms which best correspond at any given moment to the manifest strivings of all." To religious thinkers like Buber, it is to Kropotkin and the mature Proudhon that one looks for a utopianism that is created in the here and now. Human beings create "the space now possible for the thing for which we are striving, so that it may come to fulfillment *then*."[24] This revolutionary continuity means that the event that is called the revolution sets free and extends a reality that has already developed to its true possibilities. Buber stresses the community content. In Novak's terms, Buber particularly appreciates mediating structures. To the socialist Buber, society is a "living and life-giving collaboration, an essentially autonomous consociation of human beings, shaping and reshaping itself from within."[25] One can hope that the Soviets evolve in this direction, and recent events provide a mixed basis for such hope. But the false choice between "democratic capitalism" and Soviet communism does not have to be made. The prophetic tradition calls on persons and communities to go beyond both and certainly to speak out against the structural injustices of the system in which they live.

A just and human community, Buber thought, is not possible under a capitalism that denies most people autonomy. "Under capitalist economy and the State peculiar to it the constitution of society was being continually hollowed out, so that the modern individualizing process finished up as a process of atomization."[26]

That global capitalism destroyed old organic forms and in its laissez-faire version would leave individuals defenseless may be echoed in some aspects in Soviet communism, but this hardly provides direction for American society. As Buber told a socialist gathering in 1928:

> There can be pseudo-realization of socialism, where the real life of man to man is but little changed. . . . The real living together of man with man can only thrive where people have the real things of their common life in common; where they can experience, discuss and administer them together; where real fellowships and real work guilds exist. We learn more or less from the Russian attempt at realization that human relationships render essentially unchanged when they are geared to a socialist centralist hegemony which rules the like of individuals did the like of the natural social groups. Needless to say we cannot and do not want to go back to primitive communism or to the corporate State of the Christian Middle Ages. We must be quite unromantic, and, living wholly in the present, out of the recalcitrant material of our own day in history, fashion a time community.

Thus one man writing in the prophetic tradition said no to communism and capitalism and embraced a participatory sense of history in which women and men built in community as co-creators with their God.

The method of understanding that has been found by liberation theologians and communities of the poor in the Third World—at home and abroad—can be stated in the words of Abraham Heschel: "to comprehend what phenomena mean, it is necessary to suspend indifference and be involved."[27]

[1]Irving Kristol, "A Capitalist Conception of Justice," in *Ethics, Free Enterprise, and Public Policy*, ed. Richard T. De George and Joseph A. Pichler (New York: Oxford University Press, 1978), 57–69.

[2]Abraham J. Heschel, *The Prophets* (New York: Harper and Row, Harper Torchbook, 1962), 1: xv. While the authors and editors of this volume value inclusive language, quoted texts from earlier writers will not be edited to reflect contemporary usage.

[3]Ibid., 4–5.

[4]Ibid., 3.

[5]Robert McAfee Brown, "Liberation as Bogeyman," *Christianity and Crisis*, April 6, 1987, 125 (italics added).

[6]Tom Blackburn, "Michael Novak, 'I Found It,' A New Faith for the Reagan Years," *Christianity and Crisis*, May 24, 1982, 147.

[7]Heschel, *The Prophets*.

[8]Some were actually communists. John L. Lewis, who organized the coal workers, went to the communists because they were only one of two groups willing to die to organize unions, the other being the radical Christian socialists. These were the ones who could be sent anywhere to organize tenant sharecroppers in the South or elsewhere.

[9]It is also true that in the United States today there are unions like the United Electrical Workers, wherein the highest union official is paid only as much as the highest-paid factory worker under a union contract. The United Electrical Workers, once the sixth-largest CIO union, is far smaller today because government and corporate leaders conspired with professional anti-communists to set up a competing union in an effort to destroy it.

[10]The gross growth in jobs are all the jobs created. The net growth is the new jobs. All of the increase in jobs paid under $14,000 a year.

[11]Poverty-zone wages are from 130 percent of the poverty level down.

[12]Maurice Dobb, *Studies in the Development of Capitalism* (New York: International Publishers, 1947), 258.

[13]Quoted by Sidney Blumenthal, "If Reagan Is Not Roosevelt, but Coolidge, Who Will Be Hoover," *Washington Post National Weekly Edition*, November 10, 1986, 35.

[14]This argument has been made *a fortiori* by Francis Fukuyama in his essay, "The End of History?" in *The National Interest* (Summer 1989): 3–35.

[15]Therborn, *Why Some Peoples Are More Unemployed Than Others: The Strange Paradox of Growth and Unemployment* (New York: Routledge Chapman & Hall, 1986), 32.

[16]Richard J. Barnet and Ronald E. Müller, *Global Reach: The Power of the Multinational Corporations* (New York: Simon and Schuster, 1974).

[17]Frances Fox Piven and Richard Cloward, *The New Class War* (New York: Pantheon, 1982), 40–41.

[18]Ibid., 41.

[19]Ibid., 43.

[20]Christopher Hewitt, cited in G. William Dumhoff, *Who Rules America Now?* (New York: Simon & Schuster, 1983), 11.

²¹See Herbert McClosky and John Zaller, *The American Ethos: Public Attitudes toward Capitalism and Democracy* (Cambridge, Mass: Harvard University Press, 1984). Finding very little support by Americans for values that range outside of either lassisez-faire liberalism ("conservatives") or democratic liberalism ("liberals"), they also find an inverse relationship between those who hold strong "democratic" values and those who hold strong "capitalist" values: "The most democratic . . . respondents . . . are critical of certain capitalist institutions and want to modify them, but their criticism stops far short of a preference for communism, socialism, or any other system that presents itself as an alternative to capitalism. Similarly, those who most strongly favor capitalism resist the broadening or extension of democratic rights, especially to new groups and new institutions, but they do not oppose, at least in general form, such democratic values as freedom, equality, and popular sovereignty" (185–186).

²²For example, Robert Reich's new book:

> The common error . . . is the rigid delineation of "us" and "them." Modern liberalism—as distinct from its more balanced New Deal ancestor—is too ready to coddle the other; modern conservatism, to defy him. Both tend to envision human encounters as blunt conflicts of interest. . . . The conservative morality tales speak of the other's strength and deviousness; the liberal morality tales, of his weakness and need. . . . The tension between a basic stance of accommodation or one of confrontation excludes the middle ground of negotiations and collaborations that both assert "our" interests and comprehend "theirs." It is here, in the premise of generally opposed interests, that the prevailing myths serve worst as guides to reality. . . . There are few encounters in which one side wins and the other loses, apart from sporting events, litigation, and quick wars on small islands. The general case is for interests to overlap, if not completely; for all parties to gain or lose together, if not all to the same extent; for each to depend on the other, if not all to the same degree and in the same encounter. This holds for international commerce as well as for international diplomacy, for dealings between managers and workers as well as dealings between the poor and the prosperous (*Tales of a New America* [New York: Times Books, 1987], 237–38).

²³Martin Buber, *Paths in Utopia*, intro. Ephraim Fischoff, trans. R. F. C. Hull (Boston: Beacon Press, 1949), 10.

²⁴Ibid., 13.

²⁵Ibid., 14.

²⁶Ibid.

²⁷Heschel, *The Prophets*, xiii.

CHAPTER 3

The Fate of the Middle "Class" in Late Capitalism

Beverly W. Harrison
Associate Professor of Christian Social Ethics
Union Theological Seminary, New York

It is gratifying to participate in a public discussion that aims at careful theological and ethical scrutiny of contemporary economic theory and ideology. While some may mourn the loss of a consensual "public philosophy"[1] in this society, the truth is that there is hardly any public dissent—even in the academy—regarding the theoretical and practical paradigms that underlie policy prescriptions and diagnoses of American[2] political and economic woes. The ostensible disarray at the level of social values is *not* accompanied by a commensurate skepticism about the reigning paradigms of neoclassical economics and of welfare liberal, neoliberal, or neoconservative political theory. Those who are unapologetically radical in their approach to social change have an awesome task before them, especially in view of the ostensibly "social scientific" viewpoints enunciated by the most powerful whom the press and media revere.

To scrutinize the claims and counterclaims of all the ardent defenders of the political economy of the United States is not a task for a single essay. There is too much to be considered concerning both the "neoconservatives" who want less political interference in market exchange and increased government expenditures only for defense, and liberals or "neoliberals" who seek a more "realistic" social interdependence in which the interests of the United States are coordinated with other capitalist, "democratic" nations. What all these mainstream (and "malestream"[3]) analysts share, and what few who take a "radical" stance acknowledge, is that neoclassical economics deserves trust.

To a radical theorist, the neoclassical economic perspective is *the* ideology par excellence of capitalist political economy. It is a theory that explains nothing more than how to assure that capitalism remains capitalism. That is, neoclassical economics demonstrates how wealth and resources may continue to function to the advantage of the minority that controls wealth and the immediate access to political power. It is an ideology because it depicts as "rational" only economic behavior that seeks the "utility maximization" characteristic of market exchange. That other motives and values might deserve priority in our action as economic agents is either unthinkable (ruled out by definition) or, worse, held to be economically "irrational." Neoclassical economic theory is itself a system of morality—and theology and ethics—masquerading as "science." Yet those who dissent from this hidden morality have a difficult task before them. For this debate concerning the ethics of economics is consistently suppressed in public discourse. Reigning economic theory makes calls for the substantive realignment of existing economic power appear as madness. Dissenters are *by definition* "unrealistic," "utopian," or "irresponsible."

The moral and religious implications of neoclassical economic theory have already been explored. The relevant point for this discussion, however, is that this "hidden consensus" on the moral and religious benevolence of our social, political, and economic system leads people to cynicism about public life, and to the sense that it makes little difference who gets elected or what political rhetoric is used. The widespread despair about the impotence of politics, and the escape into privatized values, will continue so long as basic questions about the structural relationships between economic control and political power are ruled out of public debate. Liberals, neoliberals, and neoconservatives conspire—by uncritical acceptance of neoclassical economic theory—to keep that issue from serious discussion.

This essay offers an alternative radical reading of how the political economy is affecting the lives of the vast majority in American society—those in the "middle." Such an interpretation of what is happening to the middle "class"[4] in this society is only the beginning of the broader theological and ethical analysis required. But such an analysis can illustrate how public discourse would be improved if those who control the ideological climate permitted serious radical perspectives to be widely heard.

The principle of theological and ethical interpretation employed here is one broadly invoked by Christian and other religious feminists: a "socialist-feminist liberation hermeneutic" that seeks to take seriously the concrete experience of people's lives. Particularly, it adopts a "hermeneutic of suspicion"[5] about the existing order of things. The aim is to illumine the concrete suffering of those victimized by the social orders we human beings have constructed. A "socialist-feminist hermeneutic of suspicion" accepts accountability for the "poorest of the poor"[6]—women and men of marginalized racial, ethnic, and religious cultures excluded from full social empowerment and participation by barriers of class, gender, or sexual orientation and preference. Racism, class and gender privilege, and compulsory heterosexuality constitute powerful structural constraints making people powerless, without access to the minimal conditions for human dignity. Feminist-socialist theological and ethical perspectives seek a complex, inter-structural account of human suffering and a "praxis"[7] that understands human-divine, human to human, and human-cosmic relationships holistically and critically. Such a theological ethic assumes that human life is embedded in cultural, social, political-economic, and cosmic relationships. All basic theological and moral questions are about power-in-relationship. They question what the existing power-in-relationship is, how existing power distorts and alienates relationship and community, and how persons can act together to transform social life into genuine (non-alienated) community.

This theological vision is of a world where there are no excluded ones, but such a world is hardly the present one. The current polemic against liberation theologies vacillates between the claims that it espouses violence, that it neglects the theological task of "reconciliation," and that it is too "utopian" and "unrealistic" in insisting upon policies that transform all forms of social privilege. But social violence is always pervasive (even if invisible to the powerful) wherever social injustice exists. To kill the dream of a just and inclusive society is to entrap humanity in the status quo, to render the power of religious imagination moot, and to rob persons of hope and power to act for change.

This analysis emerges from only one critical category of a feminist liberation hermeneutic: class privilege. It needs to be stressed, therefore, that the sketch of life in the middle of this society requires amplification in other directions not offered here. White racism and ethnocentricity, Christian religious imperialism, Anglo-centric European cultural hegemony, and enforced conformity to compulsory heterosexuality all contribute powerfully to the dynamics of exclusion from middle-class life. Women, especially racial-ethnic women, and their dependent children are (and increasingly will be) "the poorest of the poor" in this nation and globally. To reinterpret critically the suffering of the middle is no substitute for addressing these broader dynamics. No politics is progressive and no theology or morality genuinely liberationist if it begins and ends with class analysis. Socialist-feminists, black and Hispanic liberationists, and others have rightfully charged that the traditional "radical" social theories generated by the Euro-centered Marxist academic traditions have produced neither theory nor strategies adequate to genuine social transformation. This failure stems precisely from a refusal to take race, gender, and the control of sexuality or cultural hegemony seriously. Nor have the traditional antagonisms of the progressive secular left enabled serious attention to the distinction between alienated and transformative religion in the struggle for liberation.

Even so, it may well be that mystification of class reality is *the* trump card of those who control ideological discourse in this society. Morally speaking, the notion of "fate" used here is suspect in any ethical analysis, if only because fate cannot be resisted in action. But in the absence of a critical theory of class, the ongoing incapacitation of middle strata people does appear almost as fate. Without a broad understanding of what is happening, it is difficult to resist policies that purport to serve the interests which—we are daily assured—all decent and hard-working people should share.

Neoclassical economics provides no theory of class relations. Unlike *all* classical political economists—including Adam Smith, David Ricardo, and Karl Marx—modern mainstream economists leave such concerns to political scientists, sociologists, and other "soft" (i.e., less "scientific") social perspectives. When liberal, neoliberal, or neoconservative theorists of the political economy speak of class at all, they tend to use the term as a synonym for "social stratum."[8] Since, presumably, every society is "stratified," every society is a "class-stratified" society. By definition then, this theory of class invites us to think of class relations as a perennial, fixed, and inevitable mode of social differentiation. The chief problem with this conception of class is that it reveals nothing about the relation of human beings to political, economic, or social power.

Recently, one empirically minded sociologist discovered that 80 percent of the people in his statistically viable sample identified themselves as "middle class." Another recent survey reported that 92 percent of people told pollsters that they were members of the "middle class."[9] Yet today, no one willing to discuss poverty in the United States denies that the poor constitute a massive group. Most responsible estimates concede that not less than 20 to 23 percent of our population lives in poverty. Some of these are "working poor," but most live outside of any regular sustained wage-relation to the economy. They are often maintained by welfare or other "safety-net" provisions or by alternative improvised arrangements such as petty crime. Still, even the millions of retired persons living on social security and modest fixed retirement incomes opt for "middle class" status when asked to identify their own affiliation.

The alternative radical approach to class hardly constitutes a simple paradigmatic alternative. Radicals—including all who look to insights from Karl Marx for understanding class dynamics in society—are far from a unified mind about what constitutes the class dynamics of late monopoly capitalism. Still, what is shared is a general critical heuristic insight that was central to Marx's polemic against his contemporaries.

Christian theologians and teachers often have profoundly misrepresented Marx's views, and Christians (in the name of respect for truth) must work to avoid perpetuating these dishonest interpretations. Marx is often portrayed as a political radical whose primary aim was to overthrow capitalism and bring in a utopian "classless" society. Based on the one small political tract he co-authored, *The Communist Manifesto*, Christians often accuse Marx of wanting to foment class conflict and "create" social discontent. This is to misunderstand not only Marx but the entire intellectual context of which he was a part.

Karl Marx's basic work as an intellectual was to trace historically how societies organized basic natural resources and human labor to produce wealth. In point of fact, Marx seemed to argue that capitalism was a world-historical phase in the organization of natural, human society and that it had created some of the conditions for genuine social democracy. One may indeed criticize Marx for underestimating capitalism's problems rather than for overestimating them. Among other things, for him capitalism had spurred and accelerated the social creation of wealth and as such was a "necessary" condition for the eradication of poverty.[10] Marx did not fully anticipate the profligate power of industrial capitalism to exhaust natural resources or pollute the earth and biosphere—a point not lost on some of his latter-day followers.

Be that as it may, what Marx aimed to accomplish was a careful analysis of how capitalism worked as a total system of political economy. He was insistent that political economists should aim for a critical (demystifying) interpretation of the past and present in order to enable humanity to avoid reproducing the alienated social relations of the present. "Social theory" (to use the term Marx employed for what most of us call "social science") must be a critical science. Positivistic knowledge of human society—that is, ways of construing present social organization as "inevitable"—presently reigns. Only a critical science[11] enables persons to act effectually to improve social relations.

Marx's view of economic relations is very different from Adam Smith's, whose perspective was adopted by the mainstream defenders of capitalist political economy. To Smith, buying and selling—market relations—are the quintessential economic activities. Marx parodied this view. In a capitalist economy, market relations—buying and selling, or "business"—*appear* to be the basic economic activities. But to define economic activity this way is to misinterpret both human nature and the genuinely distinctive features of capitalism. What makes capitalism capitalism is *the ownership of the means of production by a few,* an "owning class."[12] In contrast to Adam Smith, Marx insisted that the basic distinctive human economic activity was sensuous labor, and that a humanly emancipatory approach to political economy would have to change human political economy so that humans did not literally have to sell themselves in order to live. For Marx, the "commoditization" of labor power—a process through which persons become self-alienated because they do not control their own labor power—was the defining social relation of capitalism.[13] He predicted rightly that this commoditization would penetrate all areas of social life under capitalism. And what was happening in the economic structure was mirrored socially in cultural life.

While one may disapprove of what some followers of Marx have done with his basic insights about capitalism, he was very much on target about class. He argued that antagonistic and conflictual social relations—"class conflict"—would be pervasive where the political economy of capitalism is not altered politically. He insisted that class conflict would continue to be the characterizing feature of such a political economy because some few own the means of production and the vast majority must sell their labor to survive. Marx sought to make those disadvantaged by existing class relations more precisely aware of the social arrangements that oppressed them. This was not an effort to increase class conflict but to give existing victims consciousness of the dynamics of oppression that already shaped their lives.

Of course, modern radical social theorists still debate how Marx's insights concerning class and the social reproduction of alienation should be elaborated, given the dynamic and global changes that have taken place in capitalist political economy. Antagonistic relations between nineteenth- and early twentieth-century owners and the new industrial proletariat in the central capitalist economies have undergone dramatic change. Today, advanced monopoly capitalism is in the process of realigning itself in such a way that antagonistic class relations are reproducing themselves dramatically in every society penetrated by capitalism. This only exacerbates pre-modern class alignments. Most importantly, antagonistic class lines now run not only *within* nations but *between* them.

Still, how is life in the middle of this society shaped, conditioned, and mystified by the failure to take seriously these antagonistic social relations? From a radical perspective, the "class line" runs between the few who control wealth-creating capacity and the wage-laborers who do not have the conceptual categories to name their growing powerlessness.

Nearly fifteen years ago, a young Latin American economist noted that the task of liberation theology was far more difficult in the United States than in Latin America because here it is much more difficult to see how the political and economic forces that are reshaping the lives of all Latin American peasants are also transforming the lives of every woman, man, and child in this country. From a liberation theology perspective, "critical consciousness," or awareness of subjugation and oppression, must begin with our own experience.[14] The failure to see and name pervasive class dynamics in this society is robbing middle-strata people— especially men—of the critical insight needed to become aware of their subjugation or to act creatively and effectually against human oppression. White feminist women and racial and ethnically marginated women and men have entree into the sort of critical consciousness required for active resistance to oppression. But white mainstream men, and the women who still shape their way of seeing the world primarily through white male identification, do not have such an entry point. In the absence of the sort of critical theory of class alluded to here, those growing more powerless are particularly susceptible to manipulation and to projection of their fears onto those more powerless still. That "blaming the victim"[15] is a conspicuous social dynamic in our common life, and "meanness mania"[16] a widespread social reality, is not surprising given the ideology that teaches that America is a truly "classless" society where the social antagonisms of political and economic privilege have been largely overcome. Insofar as people believe this, they are enervated. Yet, for the most part, white people in the middle do tend to believe precisely this.

To further discern the current fate of the middle class, brief attention must be given to two matters: some features of advanced monopoly capitalism that are reshaping our domestic economy in a direction that enervates people, and the ideological convictions that maintain the "invisibility" of class relations.

No one denies that capitalist political economy has been "dynamic." But the neoclassic theory of market-state transactions does not attend to the specific history of the restructuring of capital, nor to the political, social, and cultural consequences of such processes. Once again, it must be acknowledged that radical scholars are divided about how the story of capitalist political economy unfolds historically and about how to interpret the current global restructuring of this political and economic system.

There is some consensus about how the United States economy fits into the wider picture, however. Early capitalist economy in the United States developed with "advantages," first of a slave-labor system—systems of indentured labor—and later massive immigration of peoples from other nations, many fleeing the effects of the rapid dislocations of Britain's and central Europe's own industrializing process. Land and resources were abundant, and America's decentralized liberal political system favored not only "free enterprise" but the vast private acquisition of land and resources. Until the twentieth century, the United States' geopolitical remoteness from European national political conflict also favored the development of a strong and relatively independent national economy. Technological innovation fueled the dynamic shift from the family firm (upon which Adam Smith's implicit model of micro-economics was predicated) to the regional and national corporation.

Neoclassical economics is predicated on an abstract model of market exchange presupposing competition as the distinctive dynamic of capitalist economy. Radical economic historians contend, to the contrary, that the dynamic of the capitalist business unit is toward monopoly or the effort to enhance profitability through the control of markets.[17] United States economic history must be read not only as a story of the acceleration of concentrations of wealth and power but as a story of the increasing mobilization of the state in the service of existing economic power. This latter has been accomplished in spite of massive resistance from those disadvantaged by growing concentrations of wealth. A radical reading of American history recognizes that its economic history is full of crises.[18] With each crisis, the system itself undergoes structural change and centralization to enhance profitability, no matter the cost to people in terms of joblessness, bankruptcy, and loss of economic security.

There is always political resistance to this accelerated trend toward concentration of wealth and power. Progressive political struggle now and in the past has wrested concessions that mitigate the worst effects of these changes, but not without brutal struggle, as labor, racial-ethnic, and agricultural history demonstrates.[19]

In the later nineteenth and twentieth centuries, the political economy of the United States became ever more integrated into the European system of colonialism and political competition. American participation in the "world wars" of the twentieth century—which required "total mobilization"[20] of our political economy—accelerated the liaison between the national state and those sectors of capitalism that were nationally integrated. After the Second World War, the United States had the only remaining fully functional industrialized economy in the world. For over a decade, American society reaped the fruits of this historical anomaly. The high regard most Americans have for capitalism derives in large part from memories of that time of national economic prosperity. During that period, when the productive power of the United States was unrivaled, the total wealth of the society accelerated dramatically. The so-called rising standard of living created a trickle down effect which increased the economic well-being for millions.

It is undeniable that during that period the expansion of national wealth accelerated and the margin of economic security for many people in the society was increased dramatically. What is frequently forgotten is that, prior to that period, the economic position of the vast majority was profoundly precarious, and few escaped daily anxiety about money and the economic stability of the American system. The "Great Depression" of the 1930s was atypically traumatic in the United States only because it was the first nationally integrated crisis. Regional and local depressions of comparable scale have been frequent.

Significantly, this gain in national wealth became a primary source for the "myth of classlessness." Since the election of President Nixon, neoconservatives have managed an ideological triumph by creating an alternative official history about this economic prosperity. Drawing upon fear and reaction to pressure for change in the 1960s—the Civil Rights and Black Liberation movements, the Anti-Vietnam War movement, the early stirrings of women's organized efforts for justice—propagandists of the right portray American affluence as the perennial fruit of unbridled "free enterprise." In point of fact, every objective change in the living standards of citizens of the United States has come from accelerating national wealth, not from the redistribution of that wealth. Periodic national prosperity has enabled political leaders to enact legislation resisted by conservative forces. Without political pressure, growing prosperity would not have been shared to the extent that it has been.

In asking students and others to trace their family histories socially, culturally, and politically, paying close attention to those points in that history when enhanced economic security was noted, their answers frequently turn on occasions when land or home ownership or access to higher education became a reality. Just as frequently, economic shifts were recognized when new government initiatives were enacted. Policies such as G. I. loans, veterans mortgage benefits, or enhanced spending for public education were the source of these positive shifts. Yet today, the self-designated middle class largely credits private enterprise for the generalizing of prosperity. People also increasingly accept the correlative judgment that political organization and effort can *not* affect the deep injustices of our common life. The ideology of capitalist economic interest has penetrated so deeply into public discourse that even when most "liberal" presidential candidates conceive of strategies for securing economic justice, these strategies involve deepening the liaison between massive corporate wealth and the state.[21]

Meanwhile, the transnational integration of corporate power proceeds apace, fundamentally restructuring our domestic economy. The absorption of the state into this larger global capitalist system has led to a foreign policy that commits the United States to supporting reactionary political forces in other nations that submerge their national economies in the global capitalist system. This places the United States in the position of supporting ruthless military regimes that enforce austerity on their impoverished people and that mis-develop local and national economies to serve the needs of the global system.

Our domestic economy is also undergoing profound mis-development. The much discussed problem of deindustrialization —the loss of basic industries and industrial jobs—is but the tip of the iceberg. Increasingly, this economy has become militarized— shaped and sustained by massive federal expenditures on military technology and hardware. These expenditures create far fewer jobs and no wealth-producing goods or socially beneficial services. And they also negatively affect small enterprises and family farms. The centralized, capital-intensive economy is transforming the lives and economic prospects of millions of people for the worse. Many are losing farms and businesses once thought to be the secure reward of hard work and devoted effort.

Life in the work place is changing for nearly everyone, as bureaucratization accelerates and demands for so-called productivity increase. The labor market is being transformed in ways that hold little promise for the young who go deeply into debt to gain educations that once promised "upward mobility." The labor market is "segmenting"—producing a few high-income jobs for technical elites and large numbers of low-income jobs in the service and distribution sectors, for instance, in the fast food industry, in retailing, and in the repetitive "low-tech" segment of the "high-tech" economy. Many of these new jobs carry few if any of the traditional benefits and protections won by working people in earlier labor struggles. Is it any wonder that the young are often portrayed as confused, unmotivated, or lacking in traditional values? They often know intuitively that their futures will not fit the American dream, and that the traditional values of hard work and responsibility make little difference in the world in which they live. Fewer and fewer of them can look forward to home ownership, debt-free middle age, or secure retirement.

Underfunding of public-service sectors also results in job cutbacks, downward income trajectories for those who have jobs, and escalating workloads. With fewer jobs available in the industrial sector, and with regional shifts to where industrial jobs are available, organized labor has diminished power to constrain the downward trend in wages in relation to the cost of living. Corporate profit margins are at record highs. United States workers, who have long had the lowest rate of unionization of any capitalist, industrialized nation, have virtually no way to resist workplace tyranny because their access to political power is so indirect. Through the two-party system, Democrats vie with Republicans to find solutions to public problems that enhance corporate power.

All of the foregoing is taking place with little public discussion concerning how public policy decisions and the state-corporate relationship are affecting the lives of the people of this country. The culture of capitalism—making consumable things of all relationships and activities—has penetrated American life so totally that politicians speak more of the rights of consumers than of the well-being of citizens. Without a critical conception of class, individuals feel that they are largely on their own economically, and that compassion for others or concern for the common good is naive or foolish. This isolation of human beings represents a spiritual malaise that enervates people and discourages efforts to seek ways of common action. The cultural ideology of an earlier social-welfare liberalism now combines with a widespread "social amnesia" regarding past political struggles to keep the myth of a benign political economy in place. This cultural ideology that hides class reality must be addressed.

Class may be defined by antagonistic social relations between those who control wealth and have ample political power and those whose economic life is determined by episodic wages and voter participation. Class conflict of this sort can be seen pervasively in this society. Yet that conflict remains largely covert, appearing as alienation or social "anomie,"[22] resentment, addiction, and self- or other-directed anger and violence. Class mobility, so often portrayed as a distinctive feature of our political economy, is all but nonexistent. Most radical historians deny that there has been any genuine dynamic of class mobility in our history. To the contrary, the percentage of the total wealth of this society owned and controlled by the richest 2 percent of our population has risen continuously throughout our history, and in the Reagan-Bush era it has reached unparalleled proportions. Simultaneously, the total wealth owned and controlled by the poorest 20 percent of the population has dropped perceptibly. Most people in the United States who have enjoyed a greater measure of prosperity have done so because women have gone to work. The wages of working men have been tied to inflation only by labor militancy—and then only in periods of relatively high employment. And the United States has always found high rates of unemployment to be socially tolerable by comparison to other industrialized nations. Upward mobility in America is a chimera, an impression created by rising educational levels and by favorable economic conditions maintained by global political hegemony. The actual course of class mobility is as frequently downward due to loss of job stability, declining income, lower job status, and for most working people, pauperized retirement. Social welfare provisions such as social security have done far more to assure citizens' economic survival than any of the dynamics of free enterprise.

Still, a powerful cultural ideology keeps concealed the alienations of social powerlessness. Thus, political resistance often appears as spasmodic and ineffectual. Among the many progressive social theories providing a conceptual formulation for analyzing ideology, Michael Lewis suggests that central to "the culture of inequality" is the pervasive "individual as central sensibility."[23] This conviction is totally inadequate as a description of the situation in this political economy. Yet this liberal sensibility saturates cultural discourse—in church and synagogue, home and school. It is the stuff of our political rhetoric as well. Both Presidents Reagan and Bush have depicted this nation as made up of solitary individuals.

Appeals to the cultural values of home and family—so resonant in neoconservative and neoliberal discourse—aim to convince the public that any change at the cultural level will threaten domestic tranquility. It is late monopoly capitalism that today erodes the nuclear family, just as it was the acceleration of earlier industrial capitalism that outmoded the rural extended family. Yet individualistic rhetoric offers comfort in the face of deep-seated anxiety created by growing powerlessness. This cultural manipulation feeds a nostalgia for a simpler, less threatening time, but mounting evidence suggests that American homes are as likely to be battle zones as havens, and that intimate relationships are more often the victims of socioeconomic stress than sustainers of happy and upwardly mobile workers.

Because poverty, low wages, and vulnerability to rising unemployment are borne disproportionately by racial-ethnic people and divorced white women—especially those who are single parents—it is white male workers who remain somewhat isolated from the most devastating economic impacts. Most white males remain fiercely loyal to the neoconservative cultural scenario, while a healthy "hermeneutic of suspicion" about the benevolence of our political economy inoculates most victims of racism, cultural imperialism, gender subjugation, and homophobia against it. Even "liberal" feminist consciousness among women, unless it has been forged by theoretical and personal critical reflection, can readily dissipate in the face of this cultural nostalgia. This neoconservative cultural script has as great power for women as it has for unaware white males, especially when "the individual as central sensibility" correlates with sensibilities encouraged by sex-role socialization—as it does with those women who have, until now, lived largely "privatized" or "domiciled" lives.

It is the consciousness of large numbers of such men that most powerfully feeds upon the ideology of individuality and hides the truth about the anti-personal bias of society. In their deservedly acclaimed study of working men's lives, *The Hidden Injuries of Class*, Jonathan Cobb and Richard Sennett isolate this dynamic powerfully.[24] The subjects they interviewed were hard-working men who were nevertheless trapped in jobs at the lower end of the scale. Persuaded that the system is fair and that failure is the fault of the individual, they lived lives of a double consciousness. Harboring deep self-doubt, they used powerful identification with the American Dream to displace such feelings. Rigid and perfectionist in their dealings with wives and children, they sent covert messages to them that read, "do as I say but do not be as I am." Self-loathing was manifest in rare moments of candor, the result of measuring their lives by others purportedly more successful than themselves. But a more positive identification required a constant effort to find others below them—those even less deserving of success than they. The vicious circle of blame of others, perfectionist criticism directed at their wives and children, and uncritical identification with those who had "made it" trapped the daily lives of men in the demand for invulnerability, self-reliance, and achievement.

For powerless people, particularly males, deliverance from illusion or "conscientization" requires a hard and painful look at the actual way in which the system functions. It is difficult to face the truth regarding a system that has been romantically admired, particularly in the absence of deeply grounded self-respect. Yet the basis for self-respect is denied people in the work place at every turn. At least one Christian social ethicist who has looked closely at the lives of working men has described the needed pastoral strategy for liberating such men as "grief work." But such grief work must also be part of a larger strategy of communal resistance to the centralization of political and economic power and to the growing powerlessness of local communities. Without a progressive politics of renewal, without genuine options for struggle against dehumanization, people cannot learn to value their own lives or respect themselves for their efforts at survival.

The cultural mystifications of this society include historical and social "amnesia" concerning how much hard work and genuine struggle there has been to gain the rudiments of economic participation and security. Liberal rhetoric envisions a society in which those who work hard are rewarded and thus are spared the threats of poverty or downward mobility. Those who do not fit this vision are forgotten, the value of their lives denied. And so, as Michael Lewis argues, the surrogate reward of consumer goods supplants genuine equality by providing tangible evidence of "upward mobility." Interestingly, Lewis argues that the pursuit of consumer goods, Americans' purported "materialism," has little to do with gaining these goods for their own sake, but everything to do with feeding the emptiness bred by inequality.

This spiritual situation is a dangerous one. It is exacerbated by the fact that many people in the middle and at the bottom are pitted against each other by government policy requiring individual middle-income wage earners to pay the bulk of the cost for the "social safety net." The result is a moral ethos in which social contempt is rampant.

None of this will change until larger and larger numbers of people are willing to break with the prevailing cultural ideology and to run the risks of reinterpreting the realities of our political economy. Ours is a time of "friendly fascism"[25] in which any who ask genuinely critical questions will be called "communists." Still, theologically and morally concerned people must not let themselves be silenced, no matter how many waiver and rush to join the neoconservative or neoliberal ideological line.

Most needed just now is the reopening of serious public debate on extending democracy to economic life. Historically, the term "socialist" meant one who believed that political rights must be expanded to incorporate genuine participation in decisions regarding national wealth. Today, the political right has succeeded in making "socialism" a dirty word. But whether or not this word is used, the acquiescence to the current state of affairs represents a hopelessness concerning citizen and worker control of economic productive power. When this happens, people assent to captivity in a global system that benefits only the wealthy while it undermines the habitability of this planet for the overwhelming majority of the world's people.

The United States of America is distinct for virtually silencing the debate about democratizing economic life. Here, human rights mean only those few rights already granted in our liberal Constitution. They are important to those who already have assured income, but insufficient to sustain the conditions of our common humanity. Until and unless political rights come to include economic rights, the minimum physical conditions for human dignity—food, shelter, health, education, and work—the liberal political rights Americans have will be less and less secure. As it is, the freedoms of thought and speech that we celebrate in a self-congratulatory way exist largely for the powerful, while the voices of dissent are confined to the margins. To ignore or obscure this state of affairs is only to chant incantations to the gods of capitalist political economy.

---

[1]Editor's note: Professor Harrison is referring primarily to the seminar series led by the editors of this volume for the Madison Institute on the question of a "public philosophy." The central problem addressed by this seminar is that of a coherent public philosophy of the American (religious) left which avoids both sectarianism and that loose coalition of the left publicly perceived as a collection of disgruntled "interest groups."

[2]It might be more exact to think of the U.S. as the United States of *North* America. Latin Americans have rightly pointed out that they are "Americans" too in that they also live on the continent. Nevertheless, for the sake of literary convention and simplicity, the traditional forms of "American" and "America" will be used here to denote the United States of America.

[3]This term obviously reflects the feminist criticism that social analysis also has been historically dominated by men and the particular interests they bring to it.

[4]Editor's note: The ironic use of "class" here is to indicate the author's belief that the American middle strata does not form a "class" in the proper sense of the word. Further uses of this ironic sense may be assumed without repetition of the quotation marks.

[5]This term, coined by philosopher Paul Ricouer, refers to styles of interpretation that seek the meaning of phenomena in structures not in the ostensible text, but in some more "basic" structure giving rise to it. As examples of such "hermeneutics of suspicion," Ricouer cites especially Marx and Freud.

[6]"The poorest of the poor will find pasture, and the needy will lie down in safety. But your root I will destroy by famine; it will slay your survivors" (Isa. 14:30, New International Version).

[7]"Praxis" here means a reflective theory and a strategy of action.

[8]In his classic text on economics, for instance, Paul A. Samuelson cites "class barriers to opportunity" as one of the explanations for inequality, but his discussion is confined to such status matters as education and religious affiliation (Paul Samuelson, *Economics* [New York: McGraw-Hill, 1973], 807–808).

[9]Robert W. Hodge and Steven Lagerfeld, "The Politics of Opportunity," *Wilson Quarterly*, 11, no. 5, (Winter 1987): 122.

[10]By transcending the material fetters of feudal society, capitalism freed human beings from mere natural necessity, argues Marx. But the very process that unleashed tremendous technological energy now suppresses the further progress of humankind toward the "abolition of labor." "Modern bourgeois society with its relations of production, of exchange and of property, a society that has conjured up such gigantic means of production and of exchange, is like the sorcerer who is no longer able to control the powers of the nether world whom he has called up by his spells" (Karl Marx, *Selected Writings in Sociology and Social Philosophy*, eds. T. B. Bottomore and Maximilien Rubel [New York: McGraw-Hill, 1964], 138).

[11]The notion of "critical science" developed here is at least structurally similar to the systematic concept of "critical theory" developed by the Frankfurt School. Both argue for forms of social criticism based upon fundamental analyses of society.

[12]It is important to remember that Marx did not inveigh against *privately owned property* but against the private ownership of the "means of production"—of land and resources, machines, and wage-labor control, or human labor power.

[13]"Labor-power can appear upon the market as a commodity only if, and so far as, its possessor, the individual whose labor-power it is, offers it for sale, or sees it, as a commodity" (Karl Marx, *Capital*, ed. Frederick Engles [New York: The Modern Library, 1906], 186).

[14]One may note here not only the "pedagogy of the oppressed" of Paulo Freire, which seeks a "critical awareness" by looking for the real causes for things and which Freire calls "conscientization," but the inculcation of such a critical consciousness into the theology of such liberationists as Gustavo Gutierrez in his work, *A Theology of Liberation*, eds. and trans. Sister Caridad Inda and John Eagleson (New York: Orbis Books, 1973), 91–92.

[15]See William Ryan, *Blaming the Victim* (New York: Pantheon Books, 1971).

[16]See Gerald R. Gill, *The Meanness Mania: The Changed Mood* (Washington, D.C.: Published for ISEP by Howard University Press, 1980).

[17]Michael Harrington's analysis of "corporate capitalism" provides only one example. Harry Braverman, *Labor and Monopoly Capital* (New York: Monthly Review Press, 1974) and Earnest Mandel, *Marxist Economic Theory*, trans. Brian Pearce (New York: Monthly Review Press, 1968), two vols., offer related formulations.

[18]"Crises" refers here to those periods when the so-called business cycles of neoclassical economics become "depressions" and threaten the profits of existing economic units and cause profound disruptions in people's lives.

[19]For an incisive labor history from a radical perspective, see Stanley Aronowitz, *False Promises: The Shaping of American Working Class Consciousness* (New York: McGraw-Hill, 1973).

[20]This language, reflecting the complete dedication of the resources of the society to fighting a war, was used not only in Germany, but in the United States, e.g., John Jay Corson, *Manpower for Victory: Total Mobilization for Total War*, foreword Paul V. McNutt (New York: Farrar and Rinehart, 1943).

[21]Even the Roman Catholic bishops, who are on record morally as giving priority to economic justice as basic to the common welfare, adopt such a position.

[22]This term was used by sociologist Emile Durkheim to describe the pathology of advanced organic societies when diverse social functions remain isolated from one another, such as when the division of labor creates conflicts between labor and capital, and when the specialization of knowledge fragments intellectual life.

[23]Michael Lewis, *The Culture of Inequality* (Amherst: University of Massachussetts Press, 1978).

[24]Jonathan Cobb and Richard Sennett, *The Hidden Injuries of Class* (New York: Knopf, 1972), passim.

[25]Bertram Gross, *Friendly Fascism: The New Face of Power in America* (New York: M. Evans, 1980), passim.

CHAPTER 4

An Ethical Critique of Capitalism: A Canadian Perspective

Gregory Baum
Professor of Sociology and Religion
McGill University, Montreal

This essay will consider American capitalism from a Canadian perspective, an unusual task insofar as Americans do not typically solicit Canadian understandings of economic developments and their ethical implications. There are many voices in Canada, of course—different political philosophies, political parties, and attitudes toward the market economy. What makes it even more complex is that Canada as a nation lacks a clear identity. French-speaking Quebecers even wonder whether they belong to Canada at all. But what unites all Canadians and distinguishes them from Americans is the spontaneous conviction that to understand their own country they must look beyond their own borders and examine the wider network of power to which they belong and on which they depend. Canada came to be as an assembly of British colonies, including a former French colony conquered by the sword. Canadians were able to understand their situation only as they recognized their dependency first on Great Britain and later on the United States of America. To this day Canadians follow political events in the United States with great interest—often it is like watching a movie—because they realize how much their own economy and their domestic and foreign policies depend on what takes place south of the border.

Americans, on the other hand, tend to think that they can come to an understanding of their situation by looking exclusively at their own country. Because in their quest for self-understanding Americans do not look beyond their own borders, they often fail to recognize the power relations and economic ties that bind them to the rest of the world. And for this reason, they often arrive at a slightly distorted collective self-concept. Americans tend to look upon themselves as a *nation*, while in fact they constitute an *empire*. This trend deeply influences the study of history and the social sciences in America.

In sociology, the nation is often regarded as the high point of modern historical development. Talcott Parsons looked upon the nation, especially the American nation, as a self-regulating society in equilibrium. What Americans often fail to realize is that their political and economic power shapes the development of other countries, especially in Latin America, and that for this reason they cannot come to a collective self-understanding unless they look beyond their own frontiers and take into account their imperial power.

There are of course significant intellectual and political counter-trends in the United States. At this time they are often found in concerned church circles. Volumes such as this one certainly swim against the cultural mainstream by including a perspective from another country as a contribution to understanding issues of ethics and economics.

What, then, would be a normative Canadian view of contemporary capitalism? Instead of turning to political scientists or to the political parties, one significant answer may be found in the ethical critique of capitalism contained in the pastoral documents of the Canadian churches.

Since the early seventies, the Canadian churches have developed their social ethics and pursued their social ministry in ecu-

menical fashion. The churches have supported several inter-
church committees concerned with ethical evaluation of
important political and economic realities. Some of these committees mainly do research; others, such as Project North, also ac-
tively support social causes—in this case, Native land claims; others engage in public education. These committees produce
reports that are submitted to the churches and used by church
boards to formulate their critique of society and their policy recommendations. In many instances, the Canadian churches have
composed joint ecumenical documents on social justice issues
addressed to various agencies of the government. Due to this
development, there has emerged something like an ecumenical
consensus on matters economic and political.[1]

The most systematic presentation of this critical social teaching is found in the pastoral messages of the Roman Catholic
Church. Most of the points made in these documents are also
found in various statements produced by the United Church of
Canada (an ecumenical church uniting the Presbyterian and
Methodist traditions).[2] This essay will consider especially the pastoral messages of the Canadian Roman Catholic bishops.[3]

The ethical critique of capitalism emanating from these church
offices leaves the great majority of Canadian Christians cold. It is,
however, supported by a significant minority in the churches.
The radical ecclesiastical teaching is grounded in a faith-and-
justice movement with bases in grass roots Christian groups in
Canada: among the underprivileged (such as Native peoples), the
unemployed, refugees and recent immigrants, militant labor
groups and organizations, the peace movement, socialists, and
the Canadian Social Democratic Party (NDP). (The older political
parties, Conservative and Liberal, have expressed their disapproval of the new Christian orientation. So have other representatives of the establishment.)

In the public media in the United States and Canada, the
present economic debate is often presented as an argument between the older Keynesian theory and the more recent monetarist
theory. The former recommends government involvement in the
economy. The latter recommends the return to an earlier phase of
free-market capitalism, the withdrawal of government intervention, and the renewed reliance on the self-regulating power of the
market itself. Arguments in favor of monetarism are given so

much visibility in the media that one easily gets the impression that it is the one economic philosophy that inspires government policies and guides the corporations in their decisions.

Canadian church documents do not accept this analysis. They think that the emphasis on monetarism is largely a smoke screen. It is true that the government appeals to free-enterprise principles when "privatizing" publicly owned enterprises and when "deregulating" transport and communication industries. Government invokes monetarism when it cuts welfare funding. But the government shows no interest whatever in anti-trust legislation to break up giant corporations and restore the conditions for a self-regulating market through competition. Monetarism is an ideology that disguises rather than reveals the dominant economic orientation in the United States and Canada.

The churches describe the new, neoconservative orientation toward the economy quite differently. United Church documents argue that the giant transnational corporations have acquired so much power that they are able to steer the national economy and demand that the government intervene to promote their economic interests. The Catholic bishops speak of a crisis of world capitalism. They argue that the transformation of the structure of capital has created new conditions in Canada and in other parts of the world, conditions that will cause vast social suffering. The Catholic bishops follow here the analysis of Pope John Paul II in his encyclical on labor (1981).[4]

John Paul II distinguishes three phases of industrial capitalism. The early entrepreneurial phase, defined by the self-regulating market, created enormous wealth and transformed Western civilization. It was characterized by the great suffering of working men, women, and children who were at first wholly unprotected by government legislation. The second, more social, phase of industrial capitalism extended the newly created wealth to wider sections of the population. It represented a more benign form of capitalism. Economists like John Maynard Keynes recommended that government intervene in the national economy by promoting industrial development, helping industries to get over the slack period, and providing labor codes to protect workers and establish union rights.

According to John Paul II, industrial capitalism is now entering a new phase that is likely to produce suffering even greater

than the early phase. Because of new technology and the internationalization of capital, large corporations have acquired monopolistic control over the economy and thus attained the power
to force governments to give in to them. John Paul II picks up a
term "imperialism," used by Pius XI in his 1931 encyclical on the
depression, to characterize the present domination of monopoly
capitalism.[5]

Some people think that the concept of imperialism is of Marxist origin. This is incorrect. Despite the vehement anti-communist
stance taken by the Catholic church, Catholic social teaching
makes use of this term. In 1931 Pius XI argued that competition
had committed suicide and economic dictatorship had taken its
place. He argued that monopolistic or oligopolistic control of the
production of goods and the flow of money produced a new form
of imperialism, the imperialism of money. John Paul II has returned to this concept. When visiting Canada in 1984, John Paul
II uttered the following sentence in connection with the North-
South conflict: "Poor people and poor nations—poor in different
ways, not lacking food, but also deprived of freedom and other
human rights—will sit in judgment on those people who take
these goods away from them, amassing to themselves the impe-
rialistic monopoly of economic and political supremacy at the
expense of others."[6]

In their analysis of the present crisis of world capitalism, the
Canadian bishops do not use the term "imperialism." Instead
they give a more detailed analysis of what the transformation of
capital affects in Canadian society. They argue that in the Keynesian phase of capitalism, after the Second World War, the economic elite was willing to enter into an unwritten contract with
society, and that this contract included the promise of full employment, welfare legislation for those who need help, and respect for labor organization. The bishops argue that in the present
this unwritten contract is being broken. In Canada (and in the
United States) the unemployment level is very high, the welfare
system is being dismantled, and the economic establishment tries
to humiliate labor.

Without using the papal language of imperialism, the Canadian bishops describe the transformation of capital in Canada.[7]
They point to the growth of corporations, their increasing power,
and their oligopolistic impact on the economy. The bishops men-

tion the concentration of industrial, commercial, and financial institutions in certain metropolitan regions. This leads to regional disparity and the creation of underdeveloped hinterlands in Canada. According to the bishops, the same economic logic is operative in the underdevelopment of Third World hinterlands. The bishops then mention the internationalization of capital. To enhance their profit, side-step government regulation on the environment, and escape the demands of organized labor, the large corporations are now able to move capital and units of production to other parts of the world where wages are low, where workers are not allowed to organize, where safety regulations are minimal, and the environment is legally unprotected. This phenomenon leads to deindustrialization in Canada and the United States.

Then the bishops turn to a specifically Canadian development. They mention the increase in foreign ownership of Canadian industries. An economic analysis reveals that Canadian industries are largely branch plants of American corporations and that this trend is increasing. In this situation, the decisions that affect the well-being of the Canadian people are made by persons who do not live in the same country and thus have no reason to be especially concerned about Canadian society. Foreign ownership makes the Canadian economy dependent and vulnerable.

The last trend transforming the structure of capital in Canada is the new technology. The bishops argue that this development threatens to create massive unemployment and at the same time promises to humiliate labor by creating jobs that require minimal skills. While it may not be possible to stop the present technological orientation, government should insist that the enterprises that introduce automation develop employment plans and retraining programs for the workers about to be laid off.

This analysis of the transformation of capital in Canada reveals the two contradictory features of Canadian society. The Canadian bishops speak here of "a double paradox."[8] On the one hand Canada is the home of certain transnational corporations, and the government is forced to pursue domestic and foreign policies to protect them. Here Canada is involved in the imperialism of money. On the other hand a large sector of the Canadian economy is owned and steered by American corporations, and the government is unable to protect Canadian industries and Ca-

nadian people from the harmful consequences of economic dependency. Here Canada shares to a certain extent the fate of Third
World countries.

This confusing doubleness has always been the political situation of Canada. After Canada's founding as a British dominion in
1867, the Canadian elite regarded the new country as the most
successful colony and offered to help Britain rule the world. The
elite wanted Canada to be junior partner in the empire. At the
same time the Canadian economy was largely dependent on Britain. As a victim of imperialism Canada had to rely on the export
of raw material and staple goods—on fur, fish, wood, pulp, water, wheat, and later oil—and hence suffered from what contemporary political scientists call "underdevelopment." When British
economic power was waning in Canada in the 1930s, some Canadians thought that the time for an independent, self-reliant
Canadian economy had arrived. Yet the Canadian elite chose to
make themselves dependent on the economic power of American
capital. Canada was again caught in the same paradoxical situation. The elite wanted to be junior partners in the empire, and the
Canadian people suffered under an economy characterized by
dependency and underdevelopment. To this day Canada has a
weak manufacturing sector. Canadian wealth is largely derived
from the export of natural resources. To maintain a high standard
of living, Canadians seem to be selling their country piece by
piece.

Canadians of whatever political party do not look upon the
United States as a champion of the free market. The popular free
market rhetoric is a disguise. What Canadians see is a protectionist mood in the United States—in other words, opposition to free-
market ideals. The Conservative government of Canada is cur-
rently so afraid of the growing protectionism in the United States
that it advocates a free-trade agreement between Canada and the
United States. It does not want to confront the possibility of seeing Canadian goods excluded from the American market.
Through such a free-trade agreement (the government hopes),
Canada will get in under the wire when the government of the
United States tightens tariffs across the board.

Many Canadians are strongly opposed to free trade. Why
should a huge country like the United States want to open its
market and enter into a free-trade agreement with a much smaller

country like Canada, with a proportionally much smaller market? Many Canadians argue that a free-trade agreement is attractive to the United States because it will allow American companies to come into Canada, buy out the Canadian industries, and exercise powerful influence on the Canadian government. Since the American government insists that a free-trade agreement is possible only if the Canadian government ceases to subsidize Canadian farming, fishing, and other industries, many Canadians are afraid that the present Conservative government is willing to dismantle the support for the industries that have always received help from the state. Whenever a poor colony becomes independent, it is simply taken for granted that government involves itself in the promotion of production. When Canada was founded in 1867, the Conservative prime minister, Sir John MacDonald, immediately introduced a program of tariffs and subsidies called the National Economic Policy to give the new country the chance of economic survival. Today many Canadians are afraid that in a free-trade agreement the American government will demand the removal of all "unfair" government subsidies of Canadian production, including the social programs designed to help workers —such as state-sponsored socialized medicine—that have been developed out of a Canadian social philosophy that differs considerably from the American tradition. Many Canadians are afraid that a free-trade agreement would oblige the Canadian government to withdraw its support of Canadian culture, of the broadcasting system, and the publishing of periodicals and books. In a relatively small country, especially when it has two official languages, it is simply taken for granted that government supports cultural productivity. Since the United States is such a large country, and since it is physically so close to Canada, Canadian cultural industries would not be able to survive without public support.

There is wide opposition to the government's resolve to enter into a free-trade agreement with the United States. What are the corporate interests that would be served through such an agreement? The Social Democratic Party of Canada and the Canadian Labor Congress are vehemently opposed to free trade. After hearing the critique of the Canadian economy made by the churches, we are not surprised that the Christian social justice committees strongly argue against free trade between Canada and the United

States. Some official church boards have supported this critical stance. In line with the arguments presented above, these Christian groups interpret a free-trade agreement as another heavy link in the chain of economic dependency. And since economic dependency leads to political and cultural dependency, they feel that the present negotiation could lead to a loss of Canadian sovereignty.

One may conclude from the preceding observations that the Canadian church documents do not regard monetarism as the dominant philosophy guiding the political economy. They regard it rather as a disguise. The new phase of capitalism is not characterized by the withdrawal of government from the economy but on the contrary by a new and deeper involvement of government in the national economy. The power of the giant transnationals has become so great that government is forced to serve them and promote their interests. Since the transnationals exercise power over the economy, since they are able to construct or dismantle industries, since they can create employment or unemployment, since they have control over prices, the government depends on their cooperation and hence is vulnerable to blackmail. The new involvement of government in the economy has several dimensions.

First, to keep the industries in the country, government must offer ever more advantageous conditions to the transnationals. Subsidies and tax exemptions for the corporations have become enormous. Public money is here transformed into private profit. More than that, the government supports the existing corporations and attracts new investment by providing the infrastructure for the industries, especially roads, railway lines, and airports. In Canada and America, it is not the poor but the corporations who are on the public welfare rolls.

Secondly, government assumes the task of making the country more profitable for the industries and more attractive for new investment. Of primary importance here is the humiliation of the working people. What is needed is a compliant work force. While a high rate of unemployment causes suffering among those affected by it, it has a beneficial effect on the labor market. Various measures are taken, moreover, to undermine the power of organized labor. This present class war against the working people is waged not only in institutional terms. It has a cultural dimension as well. Government is interested in promoting a culture that divides labor. In the United States, a new nationalist emphasis is to bind the workers to the ambitions of the national elite, and a new sense of ethnicity is to undermine worker solidarity. The free-market ideology, handed down from on high, is to convince the people that they live in a meritocracy, that is, a society where people get what they work for and deserve. Workers must not be envious of their bosses, and poor people must not begrudge the wealth of the few because the powerful are where they are thanks to their superior talents and selfless dedication. The entrepreneurial philosophy does not account for the government's public policies but it is ideologically useful because it makes the people who have not made it in the system feel guilty. They are poor and deserve to be poor.

Thirdly, governments involve themselves in the economy by defending the economic interests of the transnationals that have power over them. One example is government intervention to support certain transnationals in the international competition between the giant corporations. Tariffs are the most obvious instance of this strategy. Another much more problematic example is the political and military involvement of the United States government in Central and South America as well as in other parts of the world to protect the economic interests of certain United States-based corporations. The American Catholic bishops' pastoral on economic justice claims that the American administration interprets the North-South conflict in terms of categories derived from the East-West conflict.[9] Cold War rhetoric serves to legitimate involvement in Latin America while actually servicing the economic interest of certain powerful corporations. The foreign policy of the United States—and in a different sense, of Canada—cannot be understood unless it is interpreted as a service rendered to the economic aims of the powerful corporations.

Fourthly, government involves itself in the economy through its military policy. Through subsidies to the arms industries and by purchasing the arms produced, the American government has poured enormous sums into the national economy. John Kenneth Galbraith has called this "military Keynesianism." Although the products of the defense industries have basically no use value, the great defenders of entrepreneurial capitalism have registered no protest against *this* government involvement in the economy.

Finally, government serves the interests of the transnationals and the economic elite by protecting law and order in society. With growing unemployment and economic destitution, with ever wider pockets of people pushed into the margin, with increasing job insecurity in the middle class, and with hopelessness creeping into the hearts of young people, the present system serves well only a shrinking sector of the population. The experience of many thus gives rise to a gap between what they actually encounter and the ideology of the dominant system. This credibility gap is dangerous. The corporations leave it to the government to protect the existing order and stop countervailing political movements. In some countries, especially in Latin America, the government exercises this function mainly through the police force. In countries with a strong liberal tradition, this peace-keeping task is exercised primarily through the promotion of ideological concepts, even though there is also increasing reliance on police action.

In this context, it is important to recognize the usefulness of Cold War rhetoric. Americans are told that to question capitalism is unpatriotic. It is important to praise the present system, to focus on the wealth it produces and on the personal freedom it allows, even if an ever-growing sector of the population has no real access to wealth or freedom. In an important sentence the Canadian Catholic bishops say that we are culturally impoverished and enslaved if we think that we have to choose between capitalism and communism. There are other possibilities. Government-supported rhetoric exercises an ideological role by disguising these other possibilities. Government here becomes the spiritual guardian of the present economic system.

There are other measures by which the government exercises its ideological role. Through the distribution of funds and the appeal to national loyalty, government encourages academic and research institutions to hire staffs defensive of the status quo and looks with suspicion on critical thought and the search for an alternative society. Through the people government honors, through the public events it organizes, through support given to certain artists, and in many other ways, government exercises an ideological function in the service of the economic elite.

The monetarist theory thus appears as a smoke screen. "Get the government off our back" is not the slogan that describes what is taking place in the country. On the contrary, in the present phase of capitalism government is much more deeply involved in the economy than ever before. Is there a name for this phase? The Canadian church documents do use a special name. It is clear, further, that they are impressed by the book *Social Analysis*, written by Joe Holland and Peter Henriot and distributed by the Jesuit Center of Concern in Washington, D.C. It suggests that this new phase in which the government is so deeply involved be called "national security capitalism."[10] In many Latin American countries the authoritarian government—military or civilian—is an instrument in the hands of an economic elite linked to certain corporate powers. In the democratic governments of developed capitalism in the United States, Canada, and in many other countries, there is increasing pressure from corporate economic power to serve their interests. To protect their expansion and their profits, government must keep the peace in the land. Critical economic ideas and countervailing political trends must be held back. As the ideological instruments become less convincing, government demands loyalty and conformity in the name of national security. The harnessing of government to protect the interests of corporate capitalism, not monetarism, is the ruling political philosophy of our day.[11]

What remains for discussion in this context is to clarify the theological method used by the Canadian bishops and to show how this has allowed them to enter the public debate in their country. First, however, a few words of explanation are in order to indicate why the Canadian Catholic bishops have arrived at a more radical critique of the present economic system than the American Catholic bishops. The American pastoral on economic justice need not be criticized in the process. On the contrary, it deserves admiration. In fact, the American pastoral contains many radical proposals. The bishops recommend the creation of new institutions that protect people's economic rights;[12] they argue in favor of a more centralized economic planning,[13] especially relating to the production of necessities such as food and housing; and they advocate workplace democracy, that is, the extension of democratic principles into the economic sphere.[14] These are daring proposals. If they were enacted, they would initiate a qualitative transformation of capitalism. However, the principal emphasis of the American bishops' pastoral seems to be the call for a new New Deal, for a new attempt to make the Keynesian economy work. Following a sober political realism, the American bishops make ethical recommendations that could fit into an economic program worked out by a renewed Democratic Party.

The political spectrum is wider in Canada than in the United States, there being in Canada a labor-based political party (NDP) that is the heir of British socialism. It is possible, therefore, for the Canadian Catholic bishops to articulate a more radical critique of capitalism and recommend substantial surgery on the present economic system without becoming politically unrealistic or moving off into a dream world.

A brief comparison of the American and the Canadian Catholic social teaching draws attention to a significant difference in their theological methodologies. The American bishops first spelled out the biblical and Christian ethical teaching on the economy. What assignment has the Creator given to humans on this earth? What is the purpose of an economic system? How are people to exercise their joint responsibility for one another? And only after these general principles have been clarified in the light of the tradition of Catholic social teaching does the American pastoral turn to the concrete economic problems in the United States—unemployment, poverty, the farm crisis, and the relation to Third World economies.

The Canadian bishops, on the other hand, begin with a compassionate examination of the concrete historical problems and then only from the perspective acquired in this examination turn to the scriptures and the Christian tradition. They do not look for universal principles that are to be applied to particular cases; they focus instead on the particular to find the appropriate hermeneutical key for an authentic understanding of scripture and tradition in the present situation.

Because the Canadian bishops' "pastoral methodology" is so interesting, and because it can be used by Christian groups dealing with contemporary social issues, the significant paragraph from one of their pastoral documents should be quoted at some length:

> This pastoral methodology involves a number of steps; (a) being present with and listening to the experience of the poor, the marginalized, the oppressed in our society (e.g., the unemployed, the working poor, the welfare poor, exploited workers, native peoples, the elderly, the handicapped, small producers, racial and cultural minorities, etc.); (b) developing a critical anal-

ysis of the economic, political and social structures that cause human suffering; (c) making judgments in the light of Gospel social values and priorities; (d) stimulating creative thought and action regarding alternative visions and models for social and economic development; and (e) acting in solidarity with popular groups in their struggles to transform economic, political and social structures that cause social and economic injustices.[15]

A cursory reading of this paragraph reveals the impact of liberation theology and the social teaching of the Latin American bishops on the pastoral methodology of the Canadian Catholic bishops. The methodology follows the so-called option for the poor. It approaches the examination of society from the perspective of the people at the bottom and in the margin, and it gives public witness to solidarity with these groups. It studies society through its contradictions. This is the methodology that has led the Canadian bishops to the ethical critique of capitalist society. This methodology has a theological foundation, for the very starting point, the listening to the victim of society, is an act of obedience to God's Word. The biblical authority for this option for the powerless is overwhelming.[16]

At the same time, this theological starting point does not insulate the Canadian bishops from their pluralistic and largely secular society. The social scientists and political thinkers in Canada who claim to approach the study of society from an objective, value-free, "scientific" perspective have disagreed with the bishops' pastoral message, sometimes quite vehemently. But the intellectuals and politicians who approach the study of society from an emancipatory commitment, who study society in order to gain a scientific grasp of the structures of domination and to facilitate social transformation toward greater justice, have strongly supported the bishops' pastoral message. The bishops' social criticism has become part of the public debate in Canadian society.

---

[1]The history of this ecclesiastical development has not been written yet. A useful collection of Canadian church documents is John R. William's *Canadian Churches and Social Justice* (Toronto: James Lorimer, 1984).
[2]Some documents of the United Church of Canada are contained in John R. William's book cited in note 1. The most recent document on economic justice

can be found in D. Drache and D. Cameron, *The Other MacDonald Report* (Toronto: James Lorimer, 1986).

[3]For the texts of the pastoral messages, see E. F. Sheridan, ed., *Do Justice! The Social Teaching of the Canadian Catholic Bishops* (Toronto: James Lorimer, 1987). For commentaries, see G. Baum and D. Cameron, *Ethics and Economics* (Toronto: James Lorimer, 1984), a book that includes the most recent episcopal documents, and G. Baum, "Beginnings of a Canadian Catholic Social Theory," in S. Brooks, ed. *Political Thought in Canada* (Toronto: Irwin, 1984), 49–80, partially republished in the United States as "Toward a Canadian Catholic Social Theory," *Cross Currents* 35 (Summer/Fall 1985): 242–256.

[4]See G. Baum, *The Priority of Labour: A Commentary on Labourem Exercens* (New York: Paulist Press, 1982), 321–35. The same interpretation is given in Joe Holland and Peter Henriot, *Social Analysis* (Maryknoll, N.Y.: Orbis, 1980), 46–60.

[5]*Quadragesimo anno*, n. 106, in *Seven Great Encyclicals* (New York: Paulist Pressm 1963), 153.

[6]Homily at Edmonton, Alberta, September 17, 1984. *Canadian Catholic Review*, 2 (October 1984): 62.

[7]For the following analysis see the pastoral messages, "Unemployment: The Human Costs," in *Ethics and Economics* (January 1980): 180–190, and "Ethical Reflections on the Economic Crisis," in *Ethics and Economics* (January 1983): 3–18.

[8]See *Witness to Justice*, Episcopal Commission for Social Affairs, Canadian Conference of Catholic Bishops, Ottawa, 1979, 20.

[9]"Economic Justice for All," *Origins* 16 (27 November 1986): 437, n. 262.

[10]Holland and Henriot, *Social Analysis*, 77–83.

[11]For an analysis of the strategy toward social transformation recommended in the Canadian church documents, see "Toward a Canadian Catholic Social Theory," *Cross Currents* 35 (Summer/Fall 1985): 242–256. An analysis of the deleterious impact of the present economic crisis on culture and on people's personal lives cannot be undertaken here. Still, this is a topic of great pastoral concern for church leaders in Canada and the United States. How does the manner of organizing work, production, and distribution affect the human soul? According to the American bishops, "it influences what people hope for themselves and their loved ones; it affects the way they act together in society; it influences their very faith in God" ("Economic Justice for All," n. 1).

[12]Ibid., 84, 85, 95, 96.

[13]Ibid., 303–306.

[14]Ibid., 102, 103, 288–291.

[15]Sheridan, *Do Justice!* 412–413.

[16]Readers of this volume may refer back to Norman Gottwald's article on the origins of the prophetic movement, or look forward to Dorothee Soelle's article on the Sabbath traditions for direct support of this thesis.

CHAPTER 5

God's Economy and Ours: The Year of the Jubilee

Dorothee Soelle
Professor of Christian Social Ethics
Union Theological Seminary, New York

The Lord said to Moses on Mount Sinai: "Say to the people of Israel, When you come into the land which I give you, the land shall keep a sabbath to the Lord. Six years you shall sow your field, and six years you shall prune your vineyard, and gather in its fruits; but in the seventh year there shall be a sabbath of solemn rest for the land, a sabbath to the Lord; you shall not sow your field or prune your vineyard. What grows of itself in your harvest you shall not reap, and the grapes of your undressed vine you shall not gather; it shall be a year of solemn rest for the land. The sabbath of the land shall provide food for you, for yourself and for your male and female slaves and for your hired servant and the sojourner who lives with you; for your cattle also and for the beasts that are in your land all its yield shall be for food.

"And you shall count seven weeks of years, seven times seven years, so that the time of the seven weeks of years shall be to you forty-nine years. Then you shall send abroad the loud trumpet on the tenth day of the seventh month; on the day of atonement you shall send abroad the trumpet throughout all your land. And you shall hallow the fiftieth year, and proclaim liberty throughout the land to all its inhabitants; it shall be a jubilee for you, when each of you shall return to his property and each of you shall return to his family. A jubilee shall that fiftieth year be to you; in it you shall neither sow, nor reap what grows of itself, nor gather the grapes from the undressed vines. For it is a jubilee; it shall be holy to you; you shall eat what it yields out of the field.

"In this year of jubilee each of you shall return to his property."

(Leviticus 25:1–13)

The Jewish tradition of God's rest and humans' resting unfolds in three interconnected forms: the day of rest, the Sabbath of the land, and the Jubilee Year. All three forms of resting talk about "God's economy," that is, God's will for our economic house-holding, our planning and dealing. The emphasis of the biblical understanding of economy is on labor, on those who work. The other side of economy—which we may call "production," "profit," or in modern times, "capital"—is secondary. We may discover in this passage the fundamental principle of the priority of labor over capital which the pope emphasized in "Laborem Exercens" (1983). What does the Sabbath mean? The ten com-mandments are translated into all the languages on earth, and these languages have words for "heaven," "earth," "image," and "God." Only one word is not translatable: "Sabbath," the day of rest, a holiday after six days of work—perhaps the greatest gift of the Jewish people to humanity. A Jewish theologian of our time, Abraham Joshua Heschel, asks:

What is the Sabbath? A reminder of every man's royalty; an abolition of the distinction of master and slave, rich and poor, success and failure. To celebrate the Sabbath is to experience one's ultimate independence of civilization and society, of achievement and anxiety. The Sabbath is an embodiment of the belief that all men are equal and that equality of men means the nobility of men. The greatest sin of man is to forget that he is a prince. The Sabbath is an assurance that the spirit is greater than the universe, that beyond the good is the holy. The universe was created in six days, but the climax of creation was the seventh day. Things that come into being in that six days are good, but the seventh day is holy. The Sabbath is holiness in time.[1]

According to God's words, created things are "good." But in respect to the Sabbath, the first creation account tells us that God blessed it and sanctified it (Gen. 2:3). It says that each time after six days of work, one day—interrupting the routine—is made "holy." This is only the innermost center of a whole concept of human life, of a social vision that we need and that we live on today as well. The next circle around this inner center of the sacred is the Sabbath Year. And the next wider circle is the Jubilee, of which our biblical passage talks. According to the Bible, we are called to sanctify the Sabbath, the Sabbath Year, and the Jubilee; we are the ones who can turn the time in which we live into a time of liberation. This is what "making holy" is all about. The sacred takes place in time, not after this time. During the Middle Ages, in times of heavy compulsory labor, for example, the many holidays of the saints were somewhat of a Sabbath for the people. When the Reformation cleaned up these many local saints, it destroyed a niche of freedom and carried through mercilessly a Protestant work ethic. Human beings, however, need not only the time of production and reproduction, they need "holiness in time."

In the center of Jewish life there is the celebration of rest after work, the remembrance of the creation, the meditation on that which God has made. In the Sabbath God's covenant is renewed. In the center there is the celebration wherein nobody is cooking, but eating, wherein nobody is living side-by-side, but making love with each other, and out of this center God's covenant with the earth is renewed. "The seventh year you shall let [the land] rest and lie fallow, that the poor of your people may eat; and what they leave the wild beasts may eat." (Exod. 23:11). This is said in the original version of this commandment of the Sabbath Year. In our text the rest of the land is expressed rather ecologically: the earth also shall partake in God's Sabbath. But it is especially important in the different traditions to understand the connection between human labor, respect for the earth, social behavior, and God's blessing. Labor teachings, ecology, political economy, and theology belong together. Only in this way do we understand and sanctify the Sabbath Day and the Sabbath Year. "The land shall keep a sabbath to the Lord" (Lev. 25:2). The Sabbath Year is an institution that protects the earth and its inhabitants. Two-legged and four-legged beings, plants and water, air and all elements are in need of rest, a break, a time of meditation. What if we let our chemical plants pause for a year, asking for a Sabbath for the earth? The plan of many friends in the peace movement to stop this production of madness at least for some time, to freeze it, is a plan that originates in a similar understanding of life.

The underlying notion of these Sabbath regulations in the Bible is the fact that the current owners of the land are not also its lords. "The earth is the Lord's and the fulness thereof, the world and those who dwell therein" (Ps. 24:1). The earth does not belong to those who have bought or confiscated land; it has a different owner who has been there before and who is also responsible for future generations. The instructions for the Sabbath Year in our chapter say that " 'the land shall not be sold in perpetuity, for the land is mine; for you are strangers and sojourners with me' " (Lev. 25:23). All transactions of land in ancient Israel were based on this principle, namely that the land belongs to God; the individual families and their descendants were entitled to the land, which was distributed to them at the conquest. Even if they acquired indebt- edness and lost the use of the land, they still rightly remained the holders of the land.

I would like to juxtapose this heritage next to a quotation from one of the free-enterprise system's propagandists, Paul Johnson, who traces the origins of capitalism back to the idea of freehold property as legally established in early liberalism. He says:

> The instrument of the land deed or charter, giving absolute possession of land to a private individual or private corporation, is one of the great inventions of human history. Taken in conjunction with the rule of law, it is economically and politically a very important one. For once an individual can own land absolutely, without social or economic qualification, and once his right to the land is protected—even against the state—by the rule of law, he has true security of property. Once security of property is a fact, the propensity to save—which, as Keynes noted, is exceedingly powerful in man—is enormously enhanced. Not only is it enhanced; it is translated into the propensity to invest.[2]

If you listen to the words Johnson uses, you may understand the unbridgeable difference in principle from a biblical perspec-

tive. He talks about "absolute possession"; the Bible names only
God as the "absolute owner"; Johnson talks about "security of
property"; the biblical authors claim that God is our security (cf.
Pss. 18 and 33).

The second basic thought following from the phrase "The
earth is the Lord's" is closely connected with this. Because God is
the owner of the land, humans do not need to be consumed by
troubles and burdens. Rather, they can rest and enjoy the freedom of the Sabbath. " 'Do not be anxious!' " Jesus is going to say
later in the Sermon on the Mount. " 'Do not be anxious about
your life, what you shall eat, nor about your body, what you shall
put on; for life is more than food, and the body more than clothing' " (Luke 12:22–23). This dispensing with anxiousness rests in
the knowledge that the earth is God's and not in the security of
property and our propensity to save! For the Sabbath Year, the
earth is going to bring forth enough food and seed during the
sixth year so that it is sufficient until the first harvest after the
Sabbath Year, enough even for the animals and the beasts in the
field.

I would like to interrupt myself here and reflect upon the
meaning of this biblical principle: "The earth is the Lord's." Although I would have preferred a less sexist expression, I am
proud of our Bible. Even the most skilled mental acrobatics or
brain gymnastics are not able to depoliticize this theological
statement—that the earth belongs to God—and thus to misuse it
for a naive, individualistic, transcendent Christendom. That the
heaven is God's even communists do not contest! But that the
earth belongs to God entails—as does every serious theological
statement—economic, political, and social meaning and consequence. If we take away the consequence and degrade this statement to a pure pious opinion, we are doing bad theology, one
that opposes scripture and tradition, as do some of our contemporary "court theologians" who limit the Sermon on the Mount to
the individual, taking away its urgency for a politics of peace.

Today there exist two theologies—or perhaps it is more correct to say, there exist two confessions. They are no longer con-
gruent with the confessions of the sixteenth century when Christians defined themselves as "catholic" or "protestant." Today
there is a theology of the bourgeoisie and a theology of liberation.

One recognizes bourgeois theology especially by its individualism: it views the human person as a single being who finds

comfort and peace of the soul in faith. Modern life gives all of us a hard time; the stress, competition, and the loneliness of people are overwhelming—and especially in this area, Christian religion is supposed to bring comfort and healing as deliverance from evil. In this perspective of the salvation of the individual, the kingdom of God becomes utterly secondary. "Deliver us from evil" is much more important than "Your kingdom come," although both requests belong together. The theology of the bourgeoisie is the work of the white, relatively wealthy, male-run, and also androcentricly thinking middle class. It disregards the poor masses of this earth; the hungry have a role only as objects of charity. As for the rest, problems of sexual ethics or death and dying are much more important for bourgeois theology than social, political, or economic issues.

But for about twenty years there has also been a theology that is done by people who are not white, relatively wealthy, and male—the theology of liberation. This faith is not predominantly perceived as comfort in common and often miserable lives, but as a way to live, to hope, and to act. It entails a revolution in the hearts of women and men, something like Jesus' saying to the one who has been lame for many years: " 'Rise, take up your bed, and walk!' " (Mark 2:9). Christ is not just a comforter but a changer of our life. As it happened with Jesus' first disciples, who were poor and little-educated people—most of them women—so also today communities of faith grow at the grass roots level. There a new way of living together is arising, a new way of sharing, of organizing, of celebrating, and of struggling together. In many instances this new way of life results in the experience of these Christians being despised and avoided, no longer tolerated in many professions. In the Third World, persecution, torture, and death for the sake of faith are increasing. The theology of liberation originates with the poor in the townships of South Africa, in the refugee camps in El Salvador, among the women textile workers in Sri Lanka. Nevertheless, this does not mean that liberation theology is not important for us here. We ourselves are not uninvolved in the misery that people in two-thirds of the world today suffer; rather, we are a part of the problem. The representatives of my country [Germany] at international conferences, as at the UNCTAD for example, regularly vote together with the United States against all proposals that are made by the poor countries in order to change their economic situation. We are not spectators. We are not the victims. Rather, we are the offenders who cause the misery. Therefore, the theology of liberation is not just some theological fashion that we may choose to love or leave. On the contrary, it is the expression of faith given by God also to people living in the First World who struggle towards liberation— liberation from the horrible role of bringing misery on innocent people, proclaiming death sentences on children, and oppressing the hopes of the poor through police regimes, military dictator-ships, and open war. In liberation theology, the principle "the poor are the teachers" is crucial. Thus, today we learn the most from the poor and by the poor—not technology, not knowledge, but faith and hope.

In a conversation on the situation of the peoples who are oppressed by Western countries, I recently was asked by a young Swiss teacher from where I was able to take my hope. First, I was inclined to respond to him: "From my faith in the God who al-ready once has saved a people from slavery under a military empire!" But then I realized that it was not just "my" faith that carries me. Rather, it is the faith and the hope of the poor who will not give up. As long as they do not despair and do not give up themselves, as long as they keep on struggling, we have no right to say (especially in light of an analysis that counts money and weapons but does not recognize the pride and the willingness of the oppressed to fight), "There is nothing we can do!" Winnie Mandela is a fearless, courageous, struggling woman in South Africa. Her husband, Nelson Mandela, the well-established leader of the black liberation movement, had been in prison for more than twenty years. The bloody struggle of South Africa's blacks, which has been going on for decades, can teach us hope. The poor really are the teachers!

To become a Christian in the rich First World means to break with our own world, with its values, its standards, its habits. Therefore, comfort alone is not enough; we need Christ's revolu-tion. If we want to understand the Bible, we must learn to read it with the eyes of the poor. "The earth is God's!" The poor under-stand this immediately: the earth is not the property of the United Fruit Company, nor of Standard Oil, nor of the Somoza clan; "the earth is God's" means for them that the people on earth belong to God and not to a slave master.

I return now to the central biblical passage. The third circle around the institution of the Sabbath is the Jubilee Year, the year of liberation. It is defined by a collection of legal statements regarding Israel's economy, and these statements express God's special preference for the poor, the "preferential option for the poor," as the Latin American bishops' conference in Puebla (1979) formulated it. I pick here four essential statements in regard to the economy which are ratified for the fiftieth year of liberation:

1. All slaves are to be set free.
2. All property of land has to be returned to its original owners.
3. The land shall lie fallow, as in the first Sabbath Years.
4. All debts are to be totally remitted.

These laws had a double function in Israel: on one hand, they liberated the land-owning—very often indebted—small farmers from their burdens; on the other hand, they took care of the poorest and least privileged among the people. They protected them and provided a kind of social structural "net."

One may debate whether these social laws were ever in effect, that is, were carried out, or simply represent a utopian hope. Did they really have an impact in changing reality? Yet, we cannot dismiss the fact that those laws existed as a draft of a constitution for Israel, that they are part of a sacred tradition, and are thus read and pondered even by us today. No one can tell us that this tradition of ours was nothing but beautiful, utopian dreams which the theologians like to call "eschatological," related only to the end of all time. Such a view speaks as if the great visions of the Bible—like the releasing of the debt slaves, land for the landless, swords into plowshares, the lion pasturing next to the lamb— were without any reality.

Rather, they are concrete socio-historical concepts of a better order. These social laws of ancient Israel are realistic proposals for a redistribution similar to the plans for a step-by-step disarmament that we in the peace movement today offer to our governments. The care for the needy in Israel was not just an individual effort of voluntary charity! The poor, the ones in need, the widows and the orphans, had a right to be cared for by the community, even if this right was often abridged. Their poverty was not their own fault as many are made to believe. The economic order of the covenant that God had made with Israel and that takes its real social shape in the Sabbath has its foundation in the equality of the use and distribution of goods. This finds one of its clearest expressions in the story of the manna with which God feeds the Israelites in the wilderness. God takes care of the people with food, the bread from heaven. "And the people of Israel did so; they gathered, some more, some less. But when they measured it with an omer, [the one] that gathered much had nothing over, and [the one] that gathered little had no lack; each gathered according to what [they] could eat" (Exod. 16:17–18). In God's community, the people have equal access to food according to their needs. Real misery in such a need-oriented economy could only arise when this equal and just distribution of the common goods collapsed due to natural catastrophes, or in individual accidents such as illness or death. In any case, however, the responsibility for the care of the poor was with the privileged and not with the propertyless themselves. As God led the Israelites out from under bondage, so the socially stronger should be responsible for the weaker among the people. I mention this form of community in solidarity among unequally favored people especially because we are living in a time when this very community in solidarity is falling apart. Newly arising poverty in the industrializing countries strikes the unemployed, the poorly educated or uneducated, the ones who have been rationalized away. Along with this poverty there surfaces also a new ideology that almost puts an end to the Jewish-Christian tradition of responsibility in community. The poor are poor—so it is said especially in the United States but also in France—by their own fault. The rich do not need to feel guilty; their luxury is just, good, and is helping the economy. In actuality, though, tax cuts for the rich increase their wealth, and the gap between the rich and the poor grows wider. That is all right, according to this new ideology, since it removes the poor from the sight of the rich. They are made invisible through the media.

When Ronald Reagan was asked about the continually deteriorating situation of the poor in the United States, he avoided even the word "poor" in his answer, and instead talked about the "non-rich." This linguistic wrench witnesses to a denial of reality, as if the poor were not with us, as if they were of a different race to which we relate as to strange animals in a zoo. In this situation, it is good to keep in tune with the Bible, remembering what and how it speaks about humankind and the liberation traditions that originate there. The Sabbath Year and the Jubilee Year are part of a social structure in Israel that has its starting point in the equality of human needs: everyone needs a shirt against the night frost; all have the right to food and shelter; these rights cannot be distrained. The original situation of an equitable distribution of land and food has to be reinstalled over against accidents and injuries; fresh, periodic distribution is a just demand that is destroyed in the laissez-faire economy. Just as freedom—rightly understood— means liberation from social coercions and prisons that we build ourselves, again and again, so equality means adjustment to the equality of all human beings before God. Equality needs equalization. All are in need of air and water. God's sun shines for everyone. All are created to work and to love. Hence, this is the secret of the Sabbath: again and again, every seven days, every seven years, and every seven times seven years, equality shall shine again. Precisely this real and renewed equality of needs and life chances is demonized as "leveling" by our newest right-wing ideology. Whatever is biblical is once again denounced as "communist." This is obviously nonsense in the face of a tradition some four thousand years old. Yet, it becomes clear that the Bible does not lend itself to any harmony with capitalism: You cannot serve both God and capital! (cf. Matt. 6:24). From a biblical perspective, we have to ask whether God really is not interested in this so-called leveling, whether we have the right to put the liability for poverty and misery on the victims. And we have to inquire with what kind of reasoning the elite in power resign from the responsibility of the favored for the disadvantaged, of the rich for the poor, that is, for the common good and the treaty of solidarity in society.

These social laws are necessary steps to end the situation of the war between the poor and the rich in which we live today internationally. If you are told: "That's just utopian! That has never happened before and will never be!" respond to these people with the Bible: sanctify the Sabbath, and keep the year of liberation! In Proverbs 29:18 we read: "A people without a vision is going to perish." It is a kind of self-mutilation if we no longer dare even to think our wishes and hopes, if we do not outline them in detail, if we do not spell them out politically, economically, and in regard to social legislation.

I want to give an example for these necessary, concrete requests in the face of misery; it comes from a speech that Fidel Castro delivered in the latter part of the 1980s. He responded to a reproach that Nicaragua was a threat to its neighboring countries because it was trying to export revolution. Castro said that the "producer of revolution" in Third World countries were the politics of the International Monetary Fund (IMF), the enormous foreign debt, the high interest rates, the underdevelopment, the poverty, the protectionism of the industrialized countries, and exploitation. All these factors contributed to these "unbearable conditions" undermining political stability. As a solution for the debt problem Castro proposed to remit the debts of the poorest nations and to offer generous repayment conditions for the rest. The economy of the industrialized nations could take on a part of this burden of debt.[3]

When I read that, I asked myself, why has the pope or one of our Christian governments not taken up this biblical proposal? Why do I have to hear from a communist what is written in the Bible? To remit the debts of the poorest is exactly what the Bible demands. Whenever we pray the "Our Father" and say "Forgive us our debt as we forgive our debtors" (Matt. 6:12), what insults we put on God. Most of the time we do not think of the monetary debts that others have with us. But if we did take this prayer seriously and thought of the victims of our financial policy, we would begin to remit the debts of our debtors. What happens today is nothing other than our being at the throats of the poorest countries with our financial policy. Countries that used to subsidize rice and beans in the interest of the social structure now are forced to reduce such "superfluous" social costs.

Sometimes it appears that the light of the Bible—its clarity, its simple beauty, its unvarnished truth—is no longer at home with Christians in the rich countries. Although we are able to read and write, we do not make too much use of these skills. We are spiritual illiterates. But one thing is clear: if we want to take the Bible seriously, we have to read it through the eyes of the poor. The only correct hermeneutics is the hermeneutics of the victims. When I read in the book of Nehemiah in the fifth chapter how the small farmers lament because they have increased their indebtedness and have to sell their children into slavery, exposing their daughters to the discretion and lust of the rich, then I think of

places like Indonesia, Taiwan, and many others, where the peasant girls are sold as slaves to the sex tourism of the rich, often still
as children. We understand the Bible correctly if we take seriously
this reality of our world, which we influence by our economic and
military policies. God sees the misery of the landless, the ones in
debt, the ones who have become beggars. In the book of Job, we
find a description of the miserable ones:

> Through want and hard hunger they gnaw the dry and desolate
> ground; they pick mallow and the leaves of bushes, and to warm
> themselves the roots of the broom. They are driven out from
> among [the people]; they shout after them as after a thief. In the
> gullies of the torrents they must dwell, in holes of the earth and
> of the rocks. Among the bushes they bray; under the nettles
> they huddle together. A senseless, a disreputable brood, they
> have been whipped out of the land.
>
> (Job 30:3–8)

This is the world where God calls us into the covenant with God
and to the Sabbath, a Sabbath for us, a Sabbath for the land, a
Sabbath for the poor.

In 1985, a famous physicist in West Germany, Carl Friedrich
von Weizsäcker, suggested a peace council, a council like Vatican
II on behalf of peace. This proposal failed, but out of it something
better arose. Instead of having two hundred white males aged
sixty and over talking to each other about peace, a number of
grass roots groups organized what they called the "conciliar process," in which people of faith deal with the three major issues of
faith in our time, namely, justice, peace, and the conservation of
creation. By "justice," they mean the working for a new economic
world order as proposed again and again by leaders of the Third
World. They mean fair prices for raw materials, an end to economic dictatorship, different trading conditions, and so on. By
"peace," they mean disarmament and decentralization, a power
shift away from the two superpowers by which small countries
may find their independent way of living, freed from the subjec-
tion to one of the superpowers. And by "conservation of creation," they mean to use all the productive forces—set free from
militaristic research and production—to save the earth and its
creatures from industrialism's self-imposed destructiveness. A
Sabbath for us, a Sabbath for the land, and a Sabbath for the poor

is today a matter of faith, justice, peace, and the conservation of creation, which together are the substance of faith—its criteria.

In the context of this conciliar process, I would like to ask once more: why do we need the Bible so desperately? And I will respond with a text from Paul that has nothing to do with the economy, but deals with our being possessed by the powers and politics of death, the demons, thrones, and powers that rule over us. The authorities of blindness, under whom we live today, pass themselves off in their propaganda as belonging to the realms of light—Christianity and democracy. They pretend to know "the cause of all evil," and therefore they get ready for the first strike to destroy the power of all evil. The demonic principalities and powers of which Paul speaks are much more accessible to my understanding today than they were ten years ago. I may as well call them the scientific-military-industrial complex, under whose dictatorship we live, a system that rules more relentlessly than ever before. Each of the smallest countries that fails to submit to the plans of militarization (as New Zealand tried to do) is punished, is made an example. Total control of the world market is presupposed. Every attempt at uncoupling from its mechanisms is punished by massive sanctions, like military invasions, for example. Space is going to be turned into a military arena, if the "star wars" or SDI agenda is completed. World supremacy is more and more clearly the declared goal of the largest superpower. Thanks to modern media and thus the mass manipulation of consciousness, our current situation might be even less hopeful than that of the early Christians who had to live under the power structure known as the *pax romana*.

The economics of that system was a brutal exploitation of the poor, subjugated provinces. The imperial power of Rome was built on two quite different living conditions. There was a center (the city of Rome), in which all wealth, merchandise, inventions, novelties, and luxuries were concentrated. On the periphery of the system, in the conquered provinces of North Africa, the Near East, and wide parts of Europe, there was incredible misery. No food, no shelter, no clean water, no education, no jobs, no health care were the rule. The New Testament presents the economic reality correctly. Lame, blind, sick, psychotic, and neurotic people, many of them condemned to long-term or life-long illness, appear to have been the norm rather than the exception. The economic reality of the New Testament was Roman domination: a world system of injustice in which the imperial power dictated the wheat price and destroyed any form of economic and political independence, as was evident in Rome's wars against Carthage. Wherever rebellion or insurrection arose against economic control through prices for raw and hand-manufactured materials, the Roman military was at hand to suppress bloodily the indigenous uprising. Another means of economic control was enforced taxation, and its shadows can be seen in the story of the birth of Jesus in the second chapter of the gospel of Luke.

The economic-militaristic system was set up to make the rich richer and the poor poorer. There was no "free market" for those in the dependent parts of the world, as there is none today for the sugar cane cutter in Haiti or the textile worker in Taiwan. Any form of self-organization of the impoverished was forcibly repressed by the national security system of the imperial power, often allied to the local elites—such as the Herodian king's family in Palestine, who collaborated with Roman authorities. The poor in the periphery of the imperium were increasingly dependent on the world market structured by Rome. Economic laws (which they could neither understand nor influence) ruled over them like demonic cosmological powers. In one year a family might survive, in another half of the children might starve. The New Testament reflects this powerlessness of the masses in its talk about demons, principalities, and powers.

It seems to me that today we are closer to the reality of early Christianity than in the recent past. Only now, by being exposed to the powers of death, as were people in antiquity to the demons and powers, are we able to have a hunch as to what it meant to live as Christians in the unperturbed certainty of God and in opposition to those powers of death. Only today, after a long-lived and illusory belief in progress, are we are able to comprehend what Paul and his congregations understood in the resurrection. Christ is the first-born from the dead, we read in the letter to the Colossians (1:18). But the interest of the text is not to mark Christ off from us, to put him on another unreachable pedestal, but rather to see him together with us, living under the demons of death yet in the certainty of God. Christ should not be elevated, placed in heaven; that has already taken place. Rather, we are to be elevated. We shall finally begin to live instead of creeping around under the dictatorship of the powers of death. The biblical text of the Christ hymn from the first chapter of Colossians (1:15–23) dismisses any doubt that the resurrection is an event in our present life: we do not have to wait for the resurrection until after death! "You were buried with Christ in baptism, in which you were also raised with him through faith in the working of God, who raised him from the dead" (Col. 2:12). We were dead as long as we obeyed the powers of death, as long as we oriented our life according to the demonic worldly powers of money and violence, capitalism and militarism. We were dead as long as we acknowledged the dominion of these powers that every single day that God has created demands the lives of 40,000 men, women, and children. We were dead as long as we agreed to play the game while oppressing ourselves and destroying others. We were dead because God was not near and we mistook fate for God. We were dead because we had nothing to hope for, because we did not know anybody, we did not realize that hope only grows out of the community of the weak. We were dead because we did not have a goal, and thus love could not grow, but was just wilting.

"If then you have been raised with Christ, seek the things that are above, where Christ is, seated at the right hand of God. Set your minds on things that are above, not only things that are on earth. For you have died, and your life is hid with Christ in God" (Col. 3:1–3). Our death was our idolatry, our worship of the powers of death, and idolatry here is the adoration of money (cf. Col. 3:5). Just as death happens before the biological exitus, so does life. Paul says: "You, who were dead in trespasses and the uncircumcision of your flesh, God made alive together with him [Christ], having forgiven us all our trespasses" (Col. 2:13). The resurrection from the very death that is paid for with our taxes, that we make necessary through our life-style, is an event in time. No less is the other great symbol of our religious tradition, the exodus, the marching out from the house of slavery in Egypt, an event in time. Exodus and resurrection belong together; they are two ways to name liberation. We ought not to isolate them from each other, delimiting the exodus as an outside, political, economic event that affects the people and the resurrection as a transcendent inner event concerned with the individual. If we do not remember the exodus from Egypt, our belief in the resurrec-

tion fails and turns into a post-mortal individual event that has
nothing in common with what Paul talked about. Paul perceives
the resurrection of Christ as the victory over the structural powers. In a triumphal procession Christ shows these powers totally
disarmed. Imagine all officers of the Pentagon and the Kremlin
totally disarmed, without command over any people, without the
possibility to produce new images of the enemy in their media,
without power, prestige, or money. Imagine them having to walk
in Christ's triumphal procession because their potential for threat
and power is gone. Imagine them no longer able to bribe anyone's
son with jobs, education, and privileges, because our daughters
do not want to be caressed any longer by hands that work a rifle
or push the button. Resurrection means victory over the demons
which suck the blood of the peoples as never before in history.
Resurrection means liberation from the last enemy, from death.

When is this going to be? When are the powers going to be
made powerless and reconciled; when is violent death going to
perish, and when will we no longer have to play murderers,
blood-suckers, and criminals against the wretched of this earth?
"And you," Paul says, "who once were estranged and hostile in
mind, doing evil deeds, Christ has now reconciled" (Col. 1:21f.).
How strong must Christ be if he not only liberates the elites in
power—those who push the buttons in the control towers of
death—but also reconciles all of us, the partakers, who are dependent on the demons! How strong must the Christ be who
liberates those who still believe we were able to combine
shrewdly the *pax romana* and the *pax Christi*, keeping with Christ
while yet viewing the demons as useful, as if we could combine
deterrence somehow—which no longer deters—with the Sermon
on the Mount, as if we could serve Christ and the idol of profit!

Today the first-born from the dead calls us into resistance,
into Christ's freedom from the powers. Recently, there have been
situations for me when the despair in regard to my people (who
almost half a century after the last mass murder have learned so
little), and the despair in regard to my class (the middle-class of a
rich industrialized country), has crushed my spirit. Who is going
to liberate me from this body of death, the body of my society?
Who is going to free me from the coercion to do injustice? Who is
going to save my soul, which has been made drunk by the demons and dulled by their talk shows and ensnared by their lies,

not knowing to go backward nor forward? Christ gives peace and reconciles all that is on earth and heaven. This is not just an inner peace that protects us from the deadly powers in some kind of niche; it is a real peace, that touches the powers of war because it refuses any collaboration.

Violence produces submission. In this country, many think that submission to the injustice of reigning power is non-violent, but this is just the other side of violence. We must refuse to confuse this negative side of the violence in power, namely the partaking, with any non-violence. Real freedom from violence is possible only in resistance against it, in refusal, in non-cooperation. Real freedom, the freedom of Christ, does not lie in crouching under the violence. The young people who today block driveways and access roads to the means of mass destruction, who are sentenced, who quit their careers and educations because they are felons, have been set free from the rule of the powers. Resurrection cannot be separated from insurrection.

God's economy equalizes us by celebrating God's Sabbath for all beings. We have kept this equalizing, subversive power down. We have allowed the gospel to be reduced to individualism and thus cut off Christ from our lives. We agreed to a separation of church and state and a labor division between Christ and Caesar without understanding the deepest meaning of the Word of God, namely the sisterhood and brotherhood of all people, the doing of justice, and the forgiving of debts. As God equalizes us again and again in making us beloved sons and daughters, so we shall share again and again the wealth of the earth in taking on God's work: to do justice.

---

[1] Abraham J. Heschel, *God in Search of Man: A Philosophy of Judaism* (New York: Jewish Publication Society, 1955), 417.

[2] Paul Johnson, "Is There a Moral Basis for Capitalism?," in *Democracy and Mediating Structures: A Theological Inquiry*, ed. Michael Novak (Washington, D.C.: American Enterprise Institute, 1980), 52.

Acknowledgment

God and Capitalism had its origin in a 1987 lecture series on the topic "Rich and Poor: Judeo-Christian Ethics and Market Ethics." The series was sponsored by Agenda for a Prophetic Faith, an interfaith group (Roman Catholic, Protestant, Jewish and Unitarian) of clergy and laity in and about Madison, Wisconsin.

Members of the organizing committee were: Gary J. N. Aamodt and Rev. J. Stephen Bremer, Luther Memorial Church; Rabbi Jan Brahms, Temple Beth El; Rev. Kenneth Engelman, First United Methodist Church; Rev. Max D. Gaebler, First Unitarian Society; Rev. Thomas Garnhart, University United Methodist Church (Wesley Foundation); Rev. William T. King, Covenant Presbyterian Church; Steven Morrison, Madison Jewish Community Council; Fr. Anthony J. Schumacher, Holy Mother of Consolation Church; Dr. J. Mark Thomas, Ripon College; Rev. Joanne Thomson, First Congregational Church; Fr. Stephen Umhoefer, University Catholic Center; Rev. Vernon Visick, Madison Campus Ministry, Convener; Bonnee Voss, Wisconsin Conference of Churches; Rev. Thomas Woodward, St. Francis Episcopal Church.

In 1991 the Agenda for a Prophetic Faith celebrates its tenth year as a lecture series. For more information on the series, contact Madison Campus Ministry, 731 State St. Mall, Madison, WI 53703, 608/257-1039, or Temple Beth El, 2702 Arbor Drive, Madison, WI 53711, 608/238-3123.